The Way
I See It

The Way
I See It

A Look Back at My Life
on Little House

Melissa Anderson

GUILFORD, CONNECTICUT

To buy books in quantity for corporate use
or incentives, call **(800) 962-0973**
or e-mail **premiums@GlobePequot.com.**

Library of Congress Cataloging-in-Publication Data is available on file.

ISBN 978-0-7627-5970-5

Printed in the United States of America

10 9 8 7 6 5 4 3 2 1

For
Piper and Griffin

Contents

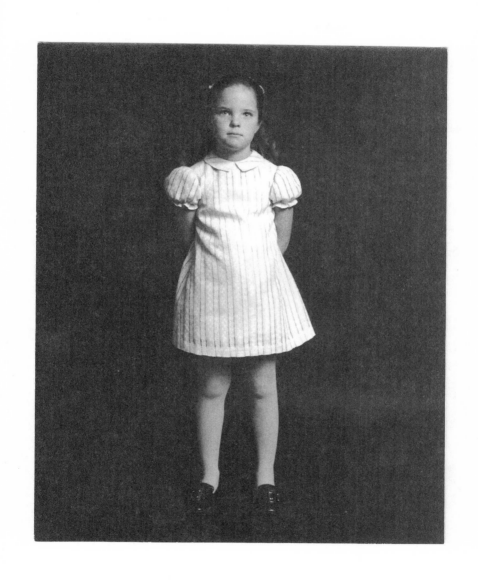

"THE WAY I SEE IT"
TEASE

FADE IN:

INT. MODERN KITCHEN — DAY

A phone hangs on the wall in this typical 1970's room. It is RINGING. A LITTLE BLONDE GIRL runs to answer it.

                    GIRL
               (calling)
          I'll get it!

She picks up the receiver and sits cross-legged on the floor, the cord hanging in loops up to the cradle.

                    GIRL
               (into phone)
          Hello?

EXT. OFFICE BUILDING — DAY

CAMERA CLOSES IN ONTO a 5th floor window.

INT. MARY GRADY'S OFFICE — DAY

MARY GRADY, a successful children's talent agent, sits at her cluttered desk, phone on her shoulder, Flair pen in her teeth. Smiles as she sing-songs into the phone:

                    MARY GRADY
          Is this Miss Melissa Sue Anderson?

INTERCUT WITH MELISSA IN HER HOUSE

                    MELISSA
                 (into phone)
        Oh, hi, Mary. How are you? Are you
        calling to send me out on an audition?

Mary goes through the clutter of photos and pieces
of paper on her desk, trying to find out what this
pilot is all about.

                    MARY GRADY
        Well, as a matter of fact, I am.
        I'm looking at the breakdown now,
        and this is what it says: "Pretty,
        blonde, blue-eyed 11-year-old girl for
        principal role in two-hour movie pilot
        for NBC." Now, this is a much bigger
        deal than the episodic television
        you've appeared in, Melissa. What do
        you think? Do you want to try?

                    MELISSA
        YES! YES! I am sooo excited! When do I
        go, Mary? What do I wear?

                    MARY GRADY
        The interview with the NBC executives
        is tomorrow afternoon, and you should
        wear something blue — it brings out
        your eyes.

                    MELISSA
        I will, Mary. And thank you. Wish me
        luck!

Mary picks up the breakdown, squinting at it.

                    MARY GRADY
        Oh, and I see here, hmmm, I think it's
        . . . a Western?

CHAPTER ONE

Too Well Fed and a Seven-Year Contract

I went to my closet to begin picking out my outfit for that first meeting at NBC, deciding on a light-blue-and-white checked shirt and my favorite pair of jeans. Mary, my agent, was right: The blue definitely brought out my eyes. After school the next day (I was in sixth grade), I went home to change my clothes, brush my hair, and use Pearl Drops Tooth Polish for an added zing to my smile.

The drive to NBC Burbank from my home in Woodland Hills should have taken about twenty minutes if there was no traffic, but as is usually the case in Los Angeles, it would take at least twice that much time. We always allowed an hour so as not to be late for these interviews. I remember seeing the big NBC logo in the parking lot and having no idea of what to expect from this meeting.

I signed myself in and sat in the outer waiting room. I don't remember seeing other girls at this meeting, but there may well have been, because as many as two hundred girls originally auditioned for each of the principal roles: Mary and Laura.

Finally, I was called to go in. The room was large and comfortable, with two sofas, some large upholstered chairs, and a large coffee table. I was led to an armchair where I sat down among a group of executives. A white-haired man with very blue eyes, the vice president of talent, held my composite (a double-sided sheet with photos and vital statistics) and began the conversation.

"Hi, Melissa. My name is Al Trescony. I have a daughter who was born on the same day as you."

I smiled. "Really? The same day as me? I've never met anyone with the same birth date."

Al laughed and said, "Well, she's a bit older, ten years, but just as pretty as you are."

"Thank you," I said.

I was nothing if not polite.

Some of the other executives in the room made small talk and asked me what I liked to do, my favorite subjects in school, my favorite sports. I said I really liked basketball. I had a hoop over my garage so I played a lot. I told them that reading and English were probably my best subjects and that I really enjoyed reading books and did a lot of it at home.

"So you've probably read the books that this movie is based on, then?" Al said.

I told him, "I don't know what books you mean. My agent said she thought it was a Western."

"Ah, well, it is, a bit," Al said. "A pioneer Western you could say: *Little House on the Prairie*?"

I bounced up and down in my chair. "I've read *all* of those books. I loved them. That's what this is? Neat!"

The executives laughed at that and asked me if I knew which role I was being considered for.

"Oh, I'm sure it must be Mary, right?"

"You got it, Melissa," Al said. "You certainly have the blue eyes for it."

Again I said, "Thank you."

As the meeting came to an end, Al said, "So, Melissa, do you think you'll be able to read for the role of Mary?"

"Absolutely," I said. "I'm so excited. It will be fun."

"All right, then. We'll be in touch with your agent about that."

We shook hands all around, and I practically skipped my way out of that room back to the reception area where my mother was waiting for me.

"Mom! It's *Little House on the Prairie!* That's the Western!"

When I got home, I pulled out my copy of *Little House on the Prairie* from my bookshelf and began to reread it, trying to envision myself in the "Mary" role, but also trying not to get my hopes up. As I turned the pages, I began to realize something—Mary doesn't do a lot. As a matter of fact, *nobody* really does very much except Laura and Pa. Mary and Ma were there, to be sure, but everything seems to revolve around Pa and Half-Pint. This was not something I, as an actress, would ever have brought up if I was lucky enough to land the role.

During the course of the series, this became a major source of conflict between Mike Landon and Ed Friendly, the other executive producer. Ed wanted to stick faithfully, if not slavishly, to the nine *Little House* books, and the pilot was based on the entire second book: *Little House on the Prairie.* Mike realized there would not be enough inherent drama if they only used the material in the books and, also, that the characters of Ma and Mary would not be fully fleshed out. He wanted the series to run for several years, at 24 episodes a year. It was a battle Mike Landon and Ed Friendly fought for quite a while. I still loved these books, though, and thought how much I and other kids would love to see a movie and TV show based on them.

At school the next day, I quickly forgot all about *Little House* and immersed myself in trying to win the "Aluminum Can Drive for Charity." I went all around my neighborhood, door-to-door, asking for aluminum cans, and even recruited my two best friends, identical twins named Pam and Tam, to help. They were great sports and even did the unthinkable with me: We donned overalls and rubber gloves and Dumpster-dove in back of some apartment buildings. Completely disgusting. But I won the Aluminum Can Drive by a mile, and better than that, Pam and Tam and I have been best friends for almost—gulp—forty years.

The following week I did, in fact, have my appointment at Paramount Studios to read for the part of Mary. I wore the same outfit that I'd worn to my NBC meeting. We actors are a superstitious bunch. If it works, we stick with it. My mother and I arrived at the studio and walked to the building that housed the production offices. It was a smallish, two-story building with narrow hallways and a narrow flight of stairs to the second level, and it was located right across the street from a courtyard that served as the exterior for the high school in *Happy Days,* which was also to be shot at Paramount.

Once again I signed in, but this time received my "sides" (pages of script to be performed or "read" in the audition)and went to a quiet place to read them over. I went in when I was called, and because it was the end of the day they got right down to business, said hello, and had me do the scene. I thought I did a good job. They seemed to like my acting, but, really, you never can tell. Again, handshakes all around and the usual "thank you"s and "we'll let you know"s. So, I was finished and we left the office.

INT. HALLWAY — DAY

Melissa and her mother exit the outer office into the hallway. A VOICE booms from behind them.

             MALE VOICE
    You're going the wrong way.

Melissa's mother turns around and practically faints.

             MOTHER
       (under her breath)
    You didn't tell me *he* was in your
    meeting!

             MELISSA
    Oh. You didn't ask me.

CONTINUED:

REVERSE ANGLE
                    MICHAEL LANDON
                (with devilish charm)
        You two *do* want to leave, don't you?

He walks toward them from the room where Melissa
has just auditioned. He is even more handsome
in person, and Melissa's mother, starstruck, is
stammering.

                      MOTHER
        Uh. Yes. Bad sense of direction.

Michael Landon looks at Melissa.

                   MICHAEL LANDON
        You did a nice job in there, kiddo.

                     MELISSA
        Thank you.

They walk down the hallway to the front entrance
to the building.

                      MOTHER
            (trying to fill the awkward silence)
        I must tell you, I've always been a
        fan of yours. We loved Bonanza.

They reach the front entrance door.

                     MELISSA
            (a premonition of things to come?)
        I loved the one where you went blind.
        But she . . .
            (pointing at her mother)
        Put me to bed in the middle of it.

EXT. BUILDING — DAY

They emerge and Landon whirls on Melissa's mother.

CONTINUED:

>   MICHAEL LANDON
>   (yelling)
>   *What?!* You did *what?!* How *could* you?!

>   MOTHER
>   Well, school and, uh, I . . .

>   MICHAEL LANDON
>   You know I'm just kidding. I liked
>   that show too. You should try to see
>   the other half, though, where I get my
>   sight back.

Melissa is looking at a pristine Jaguar E-type
12-cylinder car parked along the side of the
building.

>   MELISSA
>   Wow! Is this your car?

>   MICHAEL LANDON
>   Yep. You like it?

>   MELISSA
>   I love it. Well, thank you for walking
>   us out, Mike.

>   MICHAEL LANDON
>   Any time. Take care.

He smiles and walks to his car.

It could have all come to an end right there and then and my
mother and I could have died happy. Michael Landon was positively
dreamy.

And the audition process continued. The final hurdle I would
need to overcome was the screen test. This was new territory for me,

just as the big NBC meeting had been, but even more daunting. A screen test is exactly what it sounds like: a filmed audition of an actor or actors that will be watched by all of the decision makers. In this case, that would mean all of the NBC executives I had previously met with and all of the creative team behind *Little House,* including executive producers Michael Landon and Ed Friendly and probably some other writer/producers as well. I told myself that this was really just like when I filmed my episodes of *The Brady Bunch* and *Shaft.* The only difference was that I hadn't gotten the role yet.

My "call," the time I was to arrive at Paramount, was 7:30 a.m. for makeup and hair and 8:00 a.m. to be on set. My makeup was done by a white-haired man, aptly named Allan "Whitey" Snyder, whom I would later come to love and tease often, calling him the "Poppin' Fresh Doughboy" because of his round stomach. Larry Germain did my hair, which on that day, I believe, was just brushed and left down with a part in the middle. I had very long and shiny hair back then; I remember when my daughter Piper was eleven and twelve, her hairstyle was much the same, and that's when people said she resembled me the most.

After makeup and hair, I did not go straight to the set but rather to school. It was November, after all, and school was in session, so all of the potential Marys and Lauras (about six of each, as I recall) had to go to a little tented-off area to do our schoolwork. There was a studio teacher/welfare worker on set to oversee that all was well with any children under the age of eighteen. Every child must be accompanied by a parent or guardian and from age six can work only a total of nine hours per day, which includes lunch. Children under six can only work half that much, which is why so many television shows use identical twins to play one role, as we did with Carrie.

It's uncomfortable sitting in a waiting room with a bunch of other girls competing for the same part. It's *really* strange to sit at a table across from them and try to do your schoolwork. We all made small-talk and were cordial, of course, but talk about tension. You could cut the air with a knife. The only two girls that were actually friends seemed to be me and Tracie Savage. We had the same agent and we had always liked each other. Tracie had a very nice mom and two really talented brothers who were also actors. As an adult, I learned that Tracie had become a television reporter when I suddenly saw her standing in the pouring rain reporting on the mud slides right up the highway from where I lived in Malibu, California. I wanted to try and make my way up there to say "hi," but I was afraid she'd think I was a stalker being out in that horrible weather! I was really excited to see her reporting on the O. J. case. She was the KNBC reporter who broke the story and read the charges that were brought against him, when he had surrendered after that infamous Bronco chase.

As we sat in school, we would be called out every so often, two at a time, to go to work. We were put into pairs: one Laura and one Mary, and then we rehearsed the scene and shot it. It was a long day because there also was an additional "Laura" scene for all of the potential Lauras to do. Then they started mixing up the pairs: different Marys with different Lauras. Tracie had been auditioning for Laura, and now they had her be Mary. Well, that must be it for me, I thought. I had filmed my scene with Melissa Gilbert auditioning as Laura and was back in school, and that's where I stayed until I had finished my mandatory three hours of school.

My own children, Piper and Griffin, have both said, "Gee, Mom, you only had to go to school for three hours a day?" But three hours of what amounted to private tutoring might well have been an eternity on some days. No goofing around; no hiding to avoid being noticed. No, just serious work done in twenty-minute increments. They weren't so enamored of the idea after that.

About mid-afternoon, most of us were finished with the screen test and with school and were sent home. I believe they kept Melissa

Gilbert and another girl, so both Tracie and I were convinced that it wasn't going to be us in the pilot. My mom felt bad for us and took us out for ice cream. I'm sure she felt worse than we did. We went back to my house and had a great time playing basketball until Tracie's mother came to pick her up.

Several days passed. I remember it *seemed* like a long time since the screen test, when one evening, at dinnertime, Mary Grady called.

"What are you having for dinner?" Mary asked me.

"Oh, there's meatloaf, string beans, mashed potatoes . . ."

She interrupted, "I'm calling to let you know that they want you to play Mary, Melissa, but they . . ."

I'm sure the poor woman went deaf as I screamed into the phone, "Really? I didn't think I got it. Really??"

"Yes, yes," said Mary. "I'm sure you're excited and I am too. This is a very big deal, Melissa. There is only one thing: They think that your face is too well-fed-looking for a pioneer, and they would like to see you lose five pounds."

Silence.

"Melissa, are you there?"

"Oh, yes, Mary," I said. "I will lose five pounds. How do I do that?"

Mary replied, "Well, considering you don't need to lose weight— you really look fine just the way you are—I think you should see your doctor and ask about a really healthy way to do it."

"Okay, Mary, that's good. I can do that. I *will* do that."

I was sooo excited, especially after thinking that I hadn't gotten it. Me, who *hated* going to the doctor, couldn't wait this time.

My pediatrician agreed with Mary and said gruffly, "She's fine, just fine."

I begged, "Please, please, just five pounds, please tell me how to just lose that much and still be healthy, please!"

He finally relented and suggested that I cut out as much sugar as possible, even limiting sugary (albeit natural) fruits and juices.

Chicken and fish were okay, nothing fried, and I should beware of starches. I guess that meant no more McDonald's french fries and no more poppyseed buns on my dad's famous barbequed burgers. Oh well. It was only food. I was a serious actress. I was about to shoot my first movie for NBC. I was THRILLED!!!

While filming the series, one day the weight issue came up (probably because I lived on TAB), and Mike said he never knew anything about me losing five pounds. It must have come from Ed Friendly. All of that angst and effort and Mike never even knew??

The final step before shooting the pilot was to sign my seven-year contract in case the pilot sold and went to series. Because I was a minor, my parents had to sign *for* me.

If my parents asked me once, they asked a thousand times, was I sure I wanted to do this?

"Yes! Yes!"

I was as sure as any over-excited eleven-year-old would be. I intently tried to understand the gravity of this moment, and because I was such a serious-minded kid, I truly think that I did. I can't imagine making that kind of life-altering decision for one of my children. I know it wasn't an easy one for my parents to make and that they were torn because I wanted it so much. I, as a parent, could not have made that kind of decision for my children. I would have risked their anger and outrage and anything else they would throw at me, because I just couldn't do it.

CHAPTER TWO

The Pilot, Coogan's Law, Hives, and Whiplash

I opened the brand-new blue (my favorite color) luggage that I'd received for Christmas and happily started packing. I put in several pairs of Ditto pants, a bunch of long-sleeved T-shirts, and my favorite Wallaby shoes. I also packed the thermal underwear, sweaters, snow boots, and heavy jacket that I'd had to buy so as to be prepared to weather the weather in the northern California locations where the pilot was to be shot.

Early in January 1974, we flew up to Stockton, California, to begin the adventure that would impact my life for years (and years) to come. Stockton, or Mudville as it was once known, is located south of Sacramento and north of Modesto, California. It was the first community in California to have a name not of Spanish or Native American origin. I believe this location was chosen because it is surrounded by farmland, and in and around Stockton are thousands of miles of waterways and rivers that make up the California Delta. We needed wide-open spaces and raging rivers that we could cross with our covered wagon. The weather we encountered there was cool, about 50 degrees Fahrenheit during the day, and very rainy. We made good use of our cover set indoors when the torrential rains came.

One night, after a few days of good weather, the rains came when we weren't expecting them, and our huge trucks sank down to their axles in the mud. No wonder they called it Mudville! I reported to work early that morning to find that half of our crew had been up most of the night shoveling and trying to dig our electrical and prop/wardrobe trucks out of the mud. Kent McCray, associate producer at the time, was there, too, knee-deep in mud, shoveling with the rest of the crew. That was one of the first lessons I learned on *Little House:* Being a team player meant working together to make a great product. Copping an "attitude" or being "above" pitching in and helping out when needed was not the way this production was run.

This team of producers, staff, and most of the crew had worked together for many years, back to the *Bonanza* days. Mike Landon had worked with most of them when he directed *It's Good To Be Alive: The Roy Campanella Story* in 1973 and then brought them on to *Little House.* They really had it down; this production ran like clockwork. I found out later that Kent and Mike stockpiled any leftover money that had been budgeted for each episode. They then divided it up into envelopes and passed it out (quietly) to the crew. They were trying to ensure that these great guys and gals that worked so hard for us would stay on our show, instead of taking higher-paying jobs somewhere else. Most hour-long dramas have incredibly long days—a minimum of twelve hours, often fourteen to sixteen hours is not unusual. Longer hours mean a lot more money for a crew. Since kids were the central focus of our show, that meant scheduling our scenes inside the eight hours we could work. Any scenes that didn't have children in them would be shot after our time was up for the day. There weren't many of those, though, and Mike liked to be home for dinner with his *real* family, so "wrap" was usually not much later than 6:00 p.m.

When I first arrived in Stockton, I remember Mike telling me that he'd cast this wonderful actress to play our mother. He said she was coming from London where she'd been doing theater work and that she was just great. When we met, I could see that he was right. Karen Grassle (pronounced Grass-ley) was lovely; fresh and energetic, she was perfect for the role of Caroline. The six of us (Carrie was played by three-year-old twins Lindsay and Sydney Greenbush) all got along well and enjoyed working hard together.

Melissa Gilbert and I went to school together every day in a little trailer that was set up for us. One long wooden table and some chairs—that's about it. We each had a suitcase full of our books and assignments from our respective schools. Although we were only a year and a half apart, it could have been five. Melissa was a clever kid. She knew what worked for her. I believe she was encouraged to act as young as she could, for as long as she could. She was very nice, but we couldn't have been more different. We came from very different backgrounds; she was from a showbiz family, I was the first in mine. We were not particularly urged to be tight like sisters or best friends. I believe that was a good idea, so we would never have the "we are on the outs this week" problem so many young girlfriends do have.

I did not enjoy our schooling on the pilot because the teacher was very strict, stern, and scary, to me. I was very shy (believe it or not) and authority figures frightened me. Acting was an escape for me, a way out of just being me. I loved pretending to be someone else, and it helped me be freer with my own personality. I have always been very hard on myself, very self-critical. Acting was a relief, in a way. I was very happy to find out that we would have a different studio teacher for the series. Mrs. Minniear was terrific, the perfect combination of charm and discipline. I learned a lot from her. Helen Minniear had been Ronny (when he went by Ronny) Howard's teacher on *The Andy Griffith Show*. I think she enjoyed getting to see Ron from time to time on the Paramount lot while he was shooting *Happy Days*.

Toward the end of our time in Stockton, we shot the scene where the house is on fire and the rain comes just in time. Naturally, that day, the sky was bluer than blue, so we manufactured the rain. As I recall, there were many technical problems that afternoon, and it was growing later, darker, and colder by the minute. We finally shot the scene, and we all got absolutely drenched—I mean, soaked to the skin, and it was freezing. Once we were finished, they stuffed all of us in a couple of vans and drove us back to the honeywagons that housed our dressing rooms and dropped us off. I was so wet and cold that my entire body was shaking. Karen Grassle, just as cold and wet as I was, helped me up the steps and into my dressing room. I will never forget how kind she was to do that.

We moved along east to Sonora, California, named after the miners from Sonora, Mexico, who settled there in 1848. It is located in the beautiful Sierra Nevada foothills in the heart of California's "Gold Country." We would continue to go there to shoot at least once every season to take advantage of its historic charm—many of the city's buildings dated back to the 1800s. There was also a fantastic steam train that we used many times located nearby in Jamestown, California.

Sonora in the winter was, for me, heaven. I had grown up in suburbs near San Francisco and Los Angeles so I had really never experienced living in the snow. I had only made a few winter trips to visit my grandparents in Utah and some local trips to Big Bear Mountain to play in the snow, so I really enjoyed staying in Sonora. I also liked the little town. You could walk the main street from end to end in no time, which I did often. I guess I haven't changed much since then. I still love living in a snowy climate and being able to walk almost anywhere I need to go.

One morning, as I was sitting in the coffee shop next to the motel having breakfast, this tall, dark, and scruffy man introduced himself to me. It was Victor French, and he didn't have to tell me who he would be playing. He really did look like the Mr. Edwards described in our script, but he definitely did not act like him. Victor and Charlotte Stewart (Miss Beadle) were probably the actors most unlike the characters they portrayed. Victor was quiet and thoughtful and intellectual. Charlotte was hip and trendy and, like, totally into health food. Anyway, Victor was nice and very interesting to talk to, and we became good friends. He told me how much he was looking forward to playing a "good guy," since most of his roles had been "heavies" or bad guys. Many years later, when Mike and Kent called to tell me that he had passed away from brain cancer, I was very sad. He really was a good actor. He brought the comic relief to our show, and everyone loved him.

Mike Landon brought his wife, Lynn, and their youngest daughter, Shawna, on location with him. If they hadn't been in school, his older children would have been there as well. I think Shawna was about two, and at that time, she was a tiny terror. Having children of my own, those "twos" *are* terrible. She was adorable though, with big round eyes and blonde curls. Lynn was one of the most beautiful women I had ever seen. She was statuesque, a good bit taller than Mike, but no one would have known that because he wore lifts almost all the time back then. Our wardrobe man, Andy, said that between the lifts on the inside of his "Charles Ingalls" boots and the heels on the outside, he gained quite a few inches!

Shooting the pilot had been a great experience for me, but it was too much to hope for that it would sell and become a series. How fun would *that* be? I would have to put it out of my mind because it could be months before we'd get a yes or a no.

The pilot finished, I returned home to Los Angeles. About a week later, I auditioned for a new Disney film called *Escape to Witch Mountain*. It was a very exciting and fun script, and I had always wanted to do something for Disney. Who doesn't like Disney? In the midst of these auditions, my agent called and asked if I could ride a horse.

I started to answer, "Well, I'm . . ."

She interrupted saying, "Of course you can. What was I thinking? You just finished shooting a Western, for goodness' sake. I'll get back to you, Melissa."

It was then that I learned the first rule of Professional Acting— 101: Actors Lie. It usually starts with their representatives, as in my case, and quickly moves to the actor him/herself. See, acting gigs are hard to come by. This is not a profession you would recommend to your children. Out of the "sea" of actors, only a handful of them are working, and of that handful, only a couple of them make a living at it. It happens all the time. An actor is asked at an audition if he can swim. "Of course I can swim," says the actor. Meanwhile he is madly trying to overcome his fear of drowning. We actors are hearty, though, and we persevere like no one else. We shall overcome—practically anything—in order to GET THAT JOB.

I *did* have to horseback-ride in that Disney movie, but it turned out to be English-style riding, so it was more understandable that I might need lessons for that. And I did.

I booked *Escape to Witch Mountain* co-starring Willie Aames (who would later guest-star on an episode of *Little House*) with two conditions: one, that I take English-riding lessons two times per week, and, two, if *Little House* sold, I would not be available to shoot the movie, so it would therefore be re-cast. Willie Aames had exactly the same problem. He had just shot *Swiss Family Robinson* and was playing the waiting game just like I was. There was one more detail in this dance with Disney: We had to start "banking" school hours ASAP on the Disney lot. That meant six hours (instead of the usual three) per day, five days a week, for several weeks before shooting started. Ugh. That was going to be long. But doing that meant that we'd be available to work three extra hours each day on the movie. I'm really not sure how legal all this was, but, again, the actor's credo is: "Anything (within reason) for a job."

Time passed very slowly in that little school house on Dopey Drive. Six hours a day with two students and one teacher is interminable. Finally, one week ended on an up-note. The screening of

Little House on the Prairie was to be held on that weekend. I got all dressed up in a new yellow dress and matching coat, and went with my parents that Sunday afternoon. It was both exciting and incredibly nerve-wracking to watch myself (and so big!) on that screen. When it ended, everyone applauded and it was fun to be reunited with the cast and crew once again. The movie would air on NBC that next weekend, and everyone hoped for good ratings.

Back I went to Dopey Drive for more school. I should *really* be smart after all this, I thought.

Our pilot aired on Saturday, March 30th, 1974, and I guess we were a hit, because NBC ordered 24 episodes of *Little House on the Prairie* for the coming season. Quicker than I could say "Mickey Mouse," I was bounced off Dopey Drive at Disney and into Walnut Grove and the Little House. *Escape to Witch Mountain* would be re-cast with Kim Richards in my role and Ike Eisenmann in Willie's. You might be wondering what came of all of that schooling? I'm afraid it just made me smarter—at least, I really hope it did.

As contract negotiations were finalized between my agent and my parents, I remember hearing the words "trust fund" being used. Jackie Coogan had been a famous child star in the 1920s. His parents squandered his hard-earned money, so that by the time he reached the age of majority, he basically had nothing left. Thus "The Jackie Coogan Law" was introduced to legally protect minors earning a weekly salary. Fifteen percent of each paycheck was to be put in a trust account that could not be touched until the child reached eighteen years of age.

On May 8th, 1974 (I remember that date because it happened to be Melissa Gilbert's tenth birthday), I went to court in downtown Los Angeles to make the trust account legal and official. I remember thinking it strange that there was a birthday cake in the judge's chambers. Not very professional, I thought at the time. But the cake tasted good, as I recall. Melissa Gilbert's mother was there, as was my mother, and we all got down to business. The judge explained what all of this meant to us kids, and we nodded that yes, we understood. Then a strange thing happened: Melissa Gilbert's stepfather, a lawyer, asked to have her trust *lowered* to 10 percent. My agent, Mary, who had been through this with other child clients, remarked afterwards that she thought this was all "highly unusual" and possibly unlawful, but who were we to criticize a sitting judge? I've occasionally wondered what the other Melissa thought about this when she reached eighteen and didn't have as much money as she could (or should) have.

When NBC announced their fall schedule for the year 1974–1975, they had what was called "Breakfast with Stars" to introduce the various casts of actors to the affiliates that would be airing their series. It was hosted that year by Lloyd and Beau Bridges. When *The Other Side of the Mountain* was released in 1975, Pam and Tam and I saw it *several* times. We cried, we bawled, actually, when Beau's character "Dick Buek" dies in the plane crash. We could hardly get our little teen selves composed and together enough to leave the dark theater. We were all in love with Beau Bridges after that.

This breakfast was very exciting for me. I saw "Mr. Spock" (Leonard Nimoy), from all those *Star Trek* reruns I used to watch after school. I really wanted to meet him, but I was too

I had a chance to work with Beau Bridges in 2006 in the NBC mini-series "10.5 Apocalypse" portraying the first lady with him as the president. I told him about seeing *The Other Side of the Mountain* and what an impression he had made on me. He was very nice and appreciative and went on to tell stories about the film and the great time he had portraying the famous skier. That's a fun part of being an actress: if you hang around the business long enough, you never know who you'll work with.

shy to introduce myself. I saw Susan Saint James from *McMillan and Wife* with her beautiful long hair. And Peter Falk from *Columbo*.

The television series was supposed to start shooting in May 1974 but was pushed back to June because we were kicked out of the neighborhood in Woodland Hills, California, where we had intended to shoot our exterior scenes. That area of the San Fernando Valley was much more populated than the remote area of Simi Valley, where we ended up. The neighbors decided that huge trucks and generators at ungodly hours of the morning were just too much. Frankly, I would agree. The producers said it was a good thing, in the long run, as our Simi Valley sets could be much more spread out and, therefore, would be more realistic.

Simi Valley is forty miles north of the city of Los Angeles and was once inhabited by the Chumash Indians. The name "Simi" comes from the Chumash word *shimiji,* meaning "Valley of the Winds." It should have come from the Chumash word meaning "hot!" The average temperature from April to September is in the high 80s to mid 90s. The set of *Little House* was built on the Big Sky Ranch in the Tapo Canyon hills north of Simi Valley.

Boy, was it spread out. I can't begin to count the times I walked (or ran) up and down that road to the Little House—and even more back and forth around the "Town of Walnut Grove" sets. The makeup, hair, and wardrobe trucks were always parked up the hill and *far* away—not to mention our dressing rooms and bathrooms. It's just a good thing that the Ingallses were a poor family so we

> My husband, Michael Sloan, actually wrote my favorite *Columbo* episode of all time. It's the one with Jack Cassidy where he plays a magician. I remember seeing it when it first aired in 1976 and, of course, many, many times since in reruns. Who could imagine that I'd end up marrying the writer?

didn't have to change wardrobe *too* often. We didn't have that many dresses. We did have pinafores and the dreaded bonnets, though. I really hated my bonnet. Wearing a bonnet must be akin to wearing blinders if you are a horse—no peripheral vision. And it makes weird dents in the hair, too. Our sleeves were always supposed to be long and buttoned, but neither Melissa nor I seemed to like that very much. We almost always had them rolled up between scenes, driving both wardrobe and continuity crazy, always having to remind us to roll them back down before shooting. We either had to wear the real cotton stockings with horrible elastics that cut off circulation, or, as long as the camera couldn't see them, tights. Tights were it for me, they were much more comfortable—but in summer, *hot*. And the custom-made black boots were on *fire* in the summer as well.

A few days before we started shooting our first episode, we were to take publicity shots on our new sets in Simi Valley. I was so excited when I woke up that morning. I ran into the bathroom, took one look in the mirror, and stopped dead. I couldn't believe my eyes. My face was covered in *hives*. I was horrified. What was I going to do? How could I take publicity pictures looking like *this*? I didn't want to go to work, but, of course, I knew I had to.

All the way to the location my stomach was tied up in knots. The drive out to Simi Valley seemed like the *longest* drive of my life. In the parking lot I tried to keep my face turned away from anyone who passed. The van pulled up to take me to makeup. If the driver noticed anything—and he *had* to have noticed—he politely kept it to himself.

When we reached the top of the hill, I jumped out of the van and ran to the makeup and hairdressing trailer. I climbed up the steps and looked inside. No one else was there but Allan Snyder, our makeup man. He took one look at me and his eyes opened wide.

"What have you *done*?"

"I haven't done *anything*!" I cried. "I ate strawberries yesterday, but that's one of the only fruits I'm *not* allergic to!" When I was about seven, I was diagnosed with many severe food allergies, on top of the many others allergies I already had: house dust, grass, pollen, etc.

I was really panicked. All I could think of was Michael Landon coming into the makeup trailer to say hello, to welcome me, see how I was doing. He'd take one look at my face and I'd be back in the van on my way home. I would be *re-cast*. These were the thoughts racing through my mind.

Allan could see the panic in my eyes.

"It's all right, Missy. I'm going to fix this. Sit in the chair."

"Missy" was my nickname. When I was really little, I couldn't pronounce "Melissa"—I'd say "Missa." Over time, that became "Missy." So that's what everyone on *Little House* called me. It also distinguished me from the other Melissa.

I sat in the makeup chair, and Allan began to work his magic. By the time he'd finished, my face looked fine. He'd done a great job of covering up the offensive hives. And just in time. My previous fears were realized when the door of the makeup trailer opened and Mike climbed inside. He smiled at me, welcoming me to my first day. I half expected him to catch Allan's eye like he *knew* some wizardry had been going on in that trailer. But that didn't happen, and Allan, of course, said nothing. Mike left and I sighed with relief.

We took lots of great shots. One really nice picture of Mike and me hangs in my hallway at home. It was a fun day and a good way to ease into this new adventure.

In our first weeks of shooting, we filmed our "titles" sequence. This is where Ma and Pa come riding across the screen in the wagon and see their three girls running down the hill. Our sprinkler system had just been installed, so this hill was just starting to turn green. The wildflowers you see in the titles were *plastic* with wire stems stuck into the ground. I know this because the first time I ran down that hill, I tripped over a plastic flower and fell hard. That was my first experience with whiplash, but I still had to run down that hill all over again!

SEASON ONE
June 1974–February 1975

CHAPTER THREE

"Country Girls" and
"A Harvest of Friends"

We began shooting the series with episode number two, "Country Girls." I have no idea why we filmed out of sequence, but we shot episode number one, "A Harvest of Friends," next.

"Country Girls" was directed by William F. Claxton, who would become my favorite of our *Little House* directors. He seemed to really trust his actors, even us kids, and I liked him immediately. Bill always knew he could rely on me; he knew how seriously I took my job. He gave me added responsibilities—helping with some of the other children, and I didn't mind that at all.

One of the first scenes that we shot was the one where the other Melissa and I walk into the schoolhouse for the very first time—not just our first time in Walnut Grove, but our first time in a traditional school setting. Up to that time Laura and Mary had only been home-schooled. The set of our school/church was interesting to me. Unlike our *Little House* set, which was all real wood and solid wood furniture, this one was very fake. The pews were hollow and made of some very lightweight woodlike substance. Maybe it was balsa wood? I'm not sure, but our art department and our set decorators did a phenomenal job of staining everything to *look* like it was the real thing. Amazing. Even the Reverend Alden's pulpit looks real when you see it on screen. Walter M. (Matt, as we called him) Jeffries was our art director extraordinaire. He was famous for designing the set of the USS *Enterprise* on the original *Star Trek* series.

In this scene Nellie and Willie tease us and call us names, and watching it you can't help but feel sorry for those two little girls. Jonathan Gilbert (Melissa's brother) played Willie. He seemed to be fairly happy portraying this mean little boy, but I must say, I always wondered what he was really thinking. He was always just "the brother." That must have hurt.

Nellie Oleson was played by Alison Arngrim. Eventually, she had lots of fun being "Nasty Nellie," but when we first started working together, she was quite shy, to the point of not looking people in the eye. I can still remember Bill Claxton pleading with her: "Please, Alison, look at them while you're talking. Don't look at the ground. Look up, Alison, look up." She was adorable, especially when she still was wearing her *own* curls. When our hairdressing department found out we were a hit, they got the okay to have a wig custom-made for Alison. Trying to keep Alison's fine blonde hair in those Nellie ringlets was exhausting, I guess. I personally thought that she was much prettier with her own hair, but, of course, I never told her that.

My friend, Tracie Savage, played Christy Kennedy in the series, and that was great. When we Ingalls girls are teased in this episode, it is she who comes to our defense. I, as Mary, report back to Ma and Pa that she will probably be my best friend. Quite fitting.

I mentioned how hot it could get in Simi Valley, and during one scene in this episode, you can actually see the sweat pouring down one side of my face. If I hadn't been wearing thick Pan Stick makeup, you also would have seen how red my face was. I just recently watched this episode and found myself very surprised that this was left in and not re-shot.

"Country Girls" concludes with lovely scenes with both Caroline and Miss Beadle. It's no wonder so many of us wished to have just one teacher in our lifetime like Miss Beadle.

Mike directed "A Harvest of Friends," written by John Hawkins and William Putman, and watching it now, as I research this book, I am struck by how good a first episode it is. It has all the elements a premiere episode should have: drama, energy, pathos, heart, humor.

Pa builds our Little House and begins to work off his debt for the lumber at Hanson's Mill. He tries to get a plow and seed on credit from Oleson's Mercantile but is refused—mainly by the mean and stingy Harriet Oleson, played by Katherine MacGregor. Charles has an idea and presents an offer to the owner of the Walnut Grove Feed & Seed. He will make the much needed repairs to the roof in exchange for a plow and seed. They make a deal: as long as Charles stacks the many bags of grain as well and puts his oxen up as collateral if he doesn't finish the work. The two men shake on it and sign a contract. Now Pa has two jobs: one at Hanson's Mill and the other at the Feed & Seed, and he spends his evenings plowing his own field.

The first time we see Charles repairing the roof, we also see a man delivering some bags of grain. That man is Hal Burton, Michael Landon's stunt double. Knowing this, you can watch this episode and see just how much these two look alike. It's really uncanny. Hal was Mike's stuntman for many years and always wore cowboy boots— even off the set.

Charles keeps up this pace for quite a while and can't help falling asleep one Sunday while getting ready for church. Caroline lets him sleep, even though she is a very religious woman. She just can't bring herself to wake him. On their way home, Caroline and us girls spot Pa plowing the field. Caroline stomps her way up to him and lets him have it: "Working on the Lord's day," etc., etc.

Charles retorts, "Well, I think *God* understands farmers."

Caroline stomps back home. The music here is terrific. It punctuates Caroline's anger perfectly. David Rose, our Emmy-winning music composer was truly gifted and an irreplaceable ingredient in the mix of our show. I went to some of our music-scoring sessions.

It was fascinating to see all of the musicians playing these original scores and us up on the screen in front of them. Around the time of our "Breakfast with Stars," David invited us children to his home to see his model train. It was a real working train—just smaller. We kids could ride on it, and it was neat to think he had a train in his back-yard. Somehow you don't expect the composer of "The Stripper" to be a train enthusiast.

The story continues as Pa is very happy one day and comes home to share the news that he has worked off the lumber for the house, and he now only has one job—at the Feed & Seed. Ma mentions that maybe now he won't be quite as tired and grumpy with the kids. Nice guy that he is, he decides to devote a whole afternoon to his family. We have a picnic and an all-around nice day, until the kite Charles is flying lands in a tall tree. You can imagine what happens next: Pa climbs up to retrieve the kite, then he falls from this giant tree and breaks four ribs. Dr. Baker, always played with great sensitivity by the late Kevin Hagen, tells him that he needs weeks of rest—mostly in bed. Ma takes over the plowing duties while Charles is laid up. One day while she is out in the field, the owner of the Feed & Seed comes to take the oxen. Caroline quickly looks at the contract and tries to protest, but the heartless man leaves with his collateral.

When Charles hears about this, he immediately starts dress-ing, with great difficulty. He *must* go into town and try to deal with this situation. If he loses his crop (no oxen, no crop), then he'll lose everything. He just can't let this happen.

He looks at the contract and notices that he still has a few hours left to finish stacking the grain before he would have to forfeit his animals. Charles begins to stack the heavy bags but falls under their weight. We girls have followed him into town and start dragging the bags as best we can. The townspeople see this and quickly come to our aid. They form an assembly line and make short work of the task. Pa does not lose the oxen, and Mr. Hanson, played by Karl Swenson, asks his permission to use the Ingalls' land for the annual Plowing Contest. Now, that's a friend for ya.

Shooting the exterior scenes in Simi Valley, I felt that I was part of an exclusive club, all of us working out in the middle of nowhere, completely isolated (there were no cell phones then) from the rest of the world. It was very interesting and fun but also very dirty, and we worked some very long and physically demanding days.

Our interiors, however, were more my cup of tea. Walking into a carefully lit set for a first rehearsal is hard to describe. It's dramatic and exciting at the same time. Even as a little girl, I could feel the tradition within those huge sound-stage walls. Walking down the streets of Paramount, I could look up and see billboards for many Paramount films of the 1970s: *The Great Gatsby* starring Robert Redford, *The Conversation* with Gene Hackman, and *Chinatown*. I would later come to know the late John Alonzo, the Oscar-winning cinematographer, through Frank Sinatra Jr.

I would walk along these streets and think to myself, even at that young age, how lucky I was to have this experience and how I hoped it wouldn't end too soon. With each new episode, I learned more about acting and more about the workings of the entertainment industry. I really enjoyed it, and I soaked it up. I began to get the feeling that our *Little House* was onto something. We might be teased on late-night talk shows, but we were definitely gaining in popularity. As we say in showbiz, "As long as they spell your name right . . ."

CHAPTER FOUR

"The Love of Johnny Johnson," "Town Party, Country Party," and Eating for the Camera 101

"The Love of Johnny Johnson" starred Mitch Vogel as Johnny and was directed by Bill Claxton. Mitch Vogel was one of the many *Bonanza* alums that guest-starred on our show. Poor Mitch had to go barefoot as Johnny, but I never heard him complain—even in Simi Valley. This was a sweet episode and flattering to me as *I* was the "love." The fishing scenes in this show were shot at a lake located behind Magic Mountain (the amusement park) in Valencia, California. We used that location occasionally, whenever we needed a lake with a bit of shore around it. There was a huge water tank on the Paramount lot, but I don't think it worked well if you needed land surrounding it.

This episode was the classic unrequited love story. Laura falls hard for Johnny, and Johnny falls for Mary. I, as Mary, don't give a hoot about Johnny and have to deal with the humiliation of him carving his and my initials into the Sweetheart Tree. In real life, in a business of pretend and faux everything, it was a comfort to have that tree with those initials permanently carved there for the next eight years.

Johnny Johnson, the character, was also responsible for a major lesson in my acting life. One morning, we were filming one of our many dinner scenes. We always seemed to shoot bed scenes and dinner scenes first thing in the morning. This particular morning was great, though, because we were served fish instead of our usual Dinty Moore beef stew. Nothing against Dinty Moore, but if we ate it once, we ate it a hundred times. I loved this fish. I loved the whole dinner. It wasn't too fattening, and it was delicious.

I pretended to eat, as we all did, for the rehearsals but really dug in when we shot it. I happily ate my fish, my green beans, and drank my water.

INT. LITTLE HOUSE — NIGHT

It is suppertime and the Ingalls clan is sitting around the table enjoying the "catch of the day" — literally.

                    BILL
          And . . . Cut it! And print.

The actors start to move away from the set to relax between setups, when up runs the small but mighty MARY YERKE, Continuity/Script Lady.

                    MARY YERKE
          Missy. Missy, may I have you for a
          moment?

                    MISSY
          Sure, Mary. What's up?

Mary starts thumbing through her giant script full of notes, crossed-out sections, arrows, etc. Finds what she's looking for.

                    MARY YERKE
          Missy—Let's talk about your continuity
          for the other angles.
               (Off Missy's puzzled look)
          Of course you know, Missy, that
          you'll have to match, bite for bite,
          everything you just ate in that master
          shot. We are covering the scene in
          several angles, and it will all need
          to cut together with that original big
          Master shot.

CONTINUED:

An audible GULP comes from Missy.

                    MARY YERKE
          Let's have a seat, shall we?

CAMERA TRACKS them to some apple boxes, HOLDING as
they sit down.

                    MARY YERKE
          Let's see . . . Oh yes, here we go. On
          Caroline's line: "Well, I don't know
          where she got that idea . . . " you
          took a bite of — what *is* that you were
          eating?

                    MISSY
               (resigned; forlorn)
          Fish, Mary.

                    MARY YERKE
          Oh. Okay, you took a bite of fish, then
          a bite of green beans on Caroline's
          line: "That's right." On Laura's line:
          "Today I played Two o' Cat with the
          boys" you put your fork down, and you
          wiped your mouth with your napkin on
          her line: "And I won 'em too." Then
          you put it back on your lap. Such good
          manners you have, Missy.

                    MISSY
               (obviously overwhelmed)
          Thank you.

Mary is totally in her element. She doesn't miss a
beat.

                    MARY YERKE
          Here's where it gets tricky.

CONTINUED:

ON MISSY

Staring at her in horror — as if it already wasn't
"tricky?"

ON MARY YERKE
                    MARY YERKE
          On Laura's line about beating Johnny
          Johnson, you cut your fish, switched
          your fork back to your right hand,
          put your knife down, took a bite, and
          chewed all the way through Caroline's
          next line about being "ladylike" and
          playing "with the girls sometimes."
          Oh, and Missy, one more thing: You
          took a swallow of water on Charles's
          line: "It's good."

WIDER ANGLE ON BOTH OF THEM

Mary looks up from her script and smiles.

                    MARY YERKE
          You got all that, Missy? It's a good
          thing you're such a smart girl, and
          if you need to rehearse, don't forget,
          I'm here to help.

She gets up, moving away. CAMERA CLOSES IN ONTO
Missy, a puddle of sweat, clearly in way over her
head.

I somehow managed to memorize all of those directions just in
time to shoot the closer angles of the scene, but that was the first
and last time I would enjoy any meal in any scene, on any set, ever
again.

Alf Kjellin directed "Town Party, Country Party," and Kim Richards guest-starred.

It was nice to see Kim and her mom again. In the past, I had often seen Kim at interviews, where we might be auditioning to play sisters or sometimes even for the same role. She was a pro; she'd certainly had years of experience.

Kim Richards had been a series regular on *Nanny and the Professor,* and when I was unable to do the film *Escape to Witch Mountain,* it was she who was cast in my place. Kim was part of an acting family, and I would cross paths with them more in the future.

One hot day in Simi Valley (when wasn't it hot?), Kim and I were doing a "walk-and-talk" scene on one of the hills. We wore radio mikes hidden under our long dresses. It turned out that the sound department never intended to use any of the original dialogue spoken outside in Simi Valley, or any other exterior location, for that matter. They just needed the "guide track" that we could "loop" or replace later with cleaner-sounding identical dialogue. Actors generally hate looping. It *is* tedious. And it's very difficult to achieve the same level of performance as the original. But it's one of those things we just have to do, so I tried to enjoy the parts of the process that I liked—getting to drive the golf cart from stage 31 all the way across the lot to the looping stage and earning the reputation of "One-Take Wonder" from my good friend, sound editor Vince Gutierrez. I got really good at getting the rhythm to match my original lines. If I concentrated hard, I could get myself back into whatever scene it was and say those lines spot on. Because *Little House* was a period show, almost no original dialogue shot outside could be used. Cars, generators, airplanes—even if faintly heard—would compromise the authenticity of the program.

So, Kim and I were walking back up that hill (for the umpteenth time) to try one last rehearsal. This director was giving Kim a very hard time. He seemed to pick apart everything she did. Fortunately, the last rehearsal went well, and it was finally time to shoot.

As we walked back up, Kim started to mutter: "Gosh, does he think this is the first time I've ever done this?" "I can't believe he wants me to say it like that," and, "How do you deal with this guy?"

I answered, "Well, this is the first time we've had him as a director, so I only know as much as you, Kim."

We made it to our start marks at the top of the hill and waited.

"Action!" Alf shouted through a bullhorn, and we start.

We walked, we talked, and we did it again.

"Action!"

We walked, we talked, and we did it again.

Finally, "Cut. Print," said Alf, and as we neared the camera, we saw the *headphones* that our director was removing from his head. Oh no, I thought. He must have heard everything she said about him because our microphones were *on*. Oh. That was a lesson I would never forget. If you need to say something you don't want the whole world to hear, switch off your radio mike.

As it turned out, director Alf Kjellin did not finish this episode. Maybe he was as hard on the adults as he'd been on us? There must have been some Director's Guild rule that said that the executive producer (Mike Landon) who terminated a director could not then take over the directing duties himself, even if that executive producer was also a director and a member of the Director's Guild. Anyway, Victor French, an occasional *Little House* director, was brought in to save the day. Michael Landon was a bit of a control freak, so he couldn't *not* take over as director. He didn't technically break the rules; he *bent* them. Mike would direct the actors, the crew, the camera. He just wouldn't say "Action" or "Cut." As long as Victor was physically there to say those most important words, then all would be well.

EXT. LITTLE HOUSE — DAY

The Stand-Ins for the four girls are in place during the lighting of this scene.

                    1ST ASSISTANT DIRECTOR
          Okay, let's have the first team in for
          a rehearsal.

Missy, Tracie, Melissa, Alison, and Kim ENTER and take the places of their respective Stand-Ins. Mike ENTERS and directs the girls on where to run and play in this game of "Two o' Cat."

                    1ST A.D.
          Okay, let's have it quiet. Hey guys,
          I said quiet on the set, please. And
          . . . Mr. French.

ON VICTOR

Sitting in his Director's chair, sound asleep.

ON THE 1ST A.D.
                    1ST A.D.
          Mr. French. Victor!

ON VICTOR
                    VICTOR
              (jumps; startled)
          Huh? Oh. Action! Cut?
              (covering all the bases)
          ACTIONCUT!

And so it went, with Michael controlling and Victor directing and relishing his two most important words.

Chapter Five

"The Raccoon" and
"The Voice of Tinker Jones"

I was very happy to go to work every day but getting increasingly frustrated that I never had any really "meaty" scenes to do. I wasn't complaining; I just wanted a chance to prove I could hold my own with the best of them. It's hard to prove yourself if you never have anything written for you. And no one writes anything substantial for someone whose talent is unproven.

Finally, a writer named Joseph Bonaduce wrote me a great scene in "The Raccoon." Actually, I have a few nice scenes in this episode, but one definitely stands out.

Bill Claxton directed this show about a wild raccoon that we try to turn into our pet. It all starts with me as Mary, being responsible for Laura's favorite doll breaking. I can't afford to purchase a new head for the doll, but I stumble upon a baby raccoon to give to her instead. She adores this raccoon she names "Jasper" and trains him to do some cute tricks. One Sunday, while the family is at church, Jasper sneaks into the house, wreaks havoc, and Pa has had enough. Back to the woods the creature goes. Miraculously, the little raccoon finds his way back to the barn and Laura, and Charles relents and builds Jasper a cage. One morning we girls and Jack, our dog, go to the barn to tend to our friend. Jack makes a ruckus, excited to see the raccoon. When Laura opens the cage door, Jasper bites her, runs out, fights with Jack and bites him, too. Then the raccoon runs away, and Laura makes me promise not to tell Pa about those bites. She hopes Jasper will return once more, and if Pa knows he has bitten, he'll surely get rid of that raccoon for good. I let it slip about Jasper biting Jack, and Pa says it's a good thing he didn't tear our beloved dog apart.

The raccoon returns one night and goes after our chickens and even tries to attack Pa. It is crazed and rabid, and Charles is forced to kill Jasper. Charles and Caroline come to the realization that Jack may be infected as a result of the bite.

Early the next morning, I find Jack tied up in the barn, and Pa explains what happened. I, of course, know that *Laura* has also been bitten and have to try to break this terrible news to Pa. This scene starts with me collecting the eggs on location in Simi Valley until I hear Jack barking and walk inside the barn. The barn interior scene was subsequently filmed at the Paramount soundstage. Our barn set was quite realistic: stalls for the animals, hay bales, pitchforks, farm tools, and a ladder to climb up to the working loft. It was nice to shoot in there; I guess it was the way the cinematographer lit it. It felt warm and dramatic. Mike and I rehearsed the scene and got ready to shoot. This was a difficult scene dramatically for Mike and me, so Bill, our director, wanted absolute quiet as any last minute makeup and hair touch-ups were done. Soon everyone was ready to go.

We shot the master shot—the wide angle that takes the scene from start to finish and will be intercut with other, tighter, angles. Because my morning call was at 7:30 a.m., I was due to finish at 4:30 p.m. It was after 4:00 p.m., and there was no way we were going to be able to finish all the angles necessary to complete this scene. Helen Minniear, our welfare worker/teacher, gave her "okay" to go past the deadline to 4:45 p.m. Any more than that and she'd have to call the Board of Education for permission. Not impossible but a big deal. Mike suggested to Bill that we shoot everything with the camera in my direction first, to "shoot me out," so to speak. They could change direction and pick up the missing shots of Mike tomorrow. Bill agreed that this was probably the best thing to do, and they set up to shoot my coverage. We finished the day with my close-up; it went very well.

Mike was relieved to have the day over, as he hadn't been feeling well and just wanted to go home to bed. That was something about life on *Little House*—we were *never* too sick to work. Way too much money was at stake. I could never understand why, if we had to work, we couldn't just *use* our cold (s) or flu (s) in those episodes? But we couldn't. We just would have to loop the dialogue if we sounded too sick. My kids didn't like the sound of this too much. Staying home from school when you're sick is one of the privileges of childhood. As a matter of fact, how many occupations make *adults* work when they are sick? One of the downsides of being an actor. See, there *are* some.

Unfortunately, Mike was *really* sick. He ended up in the hospital with meningitis. He could not return to work and therefore could not finish this "Raccoon" episode. We were cutting it close regarding our air dates and episodes completed. NBC was in contact with the production staff and even Michael, from his hospital bed, as he began to recover. They were in a panic over this uncompleted episode. They were viewing it with "scene missing" where Mike's close-up should have been. Finally, and just in the nick of time, Mike told our editor, Jerry Taylor, to put the scene together using *only* the master shot and my close-up. No "scene missing" caption.

"See how it plays," he said. "I think she can carry the scene on her own."

It turns out that he was right. The network liked it, and they liked me, and what an endorsement *that* was. Most leading men wouldn't have done what he did. Mike had his faults, but egocentricity wasn't one of them, and I am reminded of this as I watch this episode.

In the timeline of the episode, our family must now play a horrible waiting game to see whether or not Jack becomes symptomatic. Chances are, if the dog doesn't show symptoms, neither will Laura. There is no treatment, no cure. I, as Mary, feel terribly guilty and responsible for so much heartache, but Laura says she still loves me, and reassures me that I'm still the "best sister" ever. Get out the Kleenex.

One night Jack is barking and jumping, and we all think the worst: rabies. Just as Charles takes aim with the rifle, Jasper, the raccoon, jumps out of the darkness! There were two raccoons; the one that killed the chickens *wasn't* Jasper. Laura runs out to the barn to release Jack from his tether, and they hug like only a little girl and her pal can.

In Alice Schroeder's *The Snowball: Warren Buffett and the Business of Life,* Buffett uses a snowball as a metaphor for his optimistic take on life. My "snowball" analogy is not optimistic like Warren's. My snowball is about an episode that began as a "not so great idea," with the hope that it will improve over time with work. As my snowball rolls down the hill, it just gets bigger and bigger. Not better. Definitely not better.

A mute metalcrafter who rides around in a wagon loaded with hanging pots and kettles is the catalyst for "The Voice of Tinker Jones."

Our Reverend Alden, always played to perfection by the late character actor Dabbs Greer, suggests that a special collection be taken toward the purchase of a church bell to "call the faithful to worship every Sunday morning." Mrs. Oleson offers to buy the bell as long as it comes with a plaque dedicating it in the Oleson's name. Some of the townspeople disagree, and an argument breaks out in the church.

Charles thinks Reverend Alden has a "war on his hands" but agrees to try to help the Reverend's plight. He will talk to the townspeople and try to get them to come to some kind of reasonable conclusion. It doesn't work, of course, and now even the children have become part of this argument.

My character says: "Fighting over a bell. I think that's silly."

All this talk about bells reminds me of a story. I recently went to see the film *The Informant!* and noticed that one of the producers was Howard Braunstein, who, along with Michael Jaffe, also produced "*10.5 Apocalypse.*" One day while we were shooting, Executive Producer Gary Pearl came up to me and said, "Melissa, today Howard Braunstein is flying up to Montreal and will be coming out to the set to meet you." I replied, "Oh, it will be good to meet him, I've seen so many of his movies." Gary went on to say that when Howard Braunstein was a young boy, he had a "crush" on me and sent me a bell. It had been printed in an article once that I had a small bell collection. It was not small after that! I received bells of all kinds from all over the world. Anyway, Gary knew that I probably wouldn't remember exactly *which* of those bells Howard sent, but could I lie and tell him I *did* remember? *Me*, lie? So, I met Howard Braunstein, along with his lovely family, and I thanked him for sending me that *beautiful* bell when we were both young(er). I saw the same gleam in his eyes that I know I had when I met Beau Bridges on that very same set.

Poor Reverend Alden thinks it best that he leave his ministering duties in Walnut Grove to put an end to this ridiculous (my word) conflict.

Karen Grassle seems to be the best part of this awful episode. She is great in a scene with Mike where she is ranting about being verbally abused by the horrible husband of one of her friends. It's just a short scene, but Karen really made the most of it.

If anyone could breathe life into "Stinker Jones," as the crew called it, Leo Penn was the guy. He was on the small side, as I recall, with grayish-whiteish hair and half glasses that he peered over. He had an abundance of energy, which is, I'm sure, one of the reasons he would have been asked to direct in this case. He was good with children, he laughed a lot, and he was a very good director.

So, Tinker decides that *he* will make the bell himself, and enlists all the children's help. We run around Walnut Grove, snatching up any metal we can find. Eventually, all of those pots, pans, pails, cans, tins, and toys will be melted down over a giant fire. Between the blazing sun, the big arc lamps (I've never understood why we had to use those lamps *outside*), and that fire, it's not hard to see how hot we all were in those scenes. We sweated off pounds, for sure. When I said that I thought Sean Penn probably had fun, I certainly hope he did, because he sure earned his paycheck that week. We *all* did.

Tinker Jones crafts a beautiful bell for the church and brings our little town back together again, and luckily our loyal viewers "kept the faith" and stuck with us.

Well, they can't *all* be Shakespeare, can they?

In a scene with all of us kids and Tinker Jones, a prominently placed Sean Penn was working as an extra (someone featured on camera but who never speaks any dialogue). I presume that it was fun for him to be able to come to work with his dad, our director, Leo Penn.

CHAPTER SIX

"The Award"

Michael Landon wrote himself out of "The Award" by having Pa and Mr. Edwards go out of town for a few weeks on business for Mr. Hanson. Perhaps one of the reasons Mike did this was so that he would have more time to deal with the ever-growing rift between himself and our other executive producer, Ed Friendly. I think it was becoming increasingly difficult for them to get along—let alone work together. Their visions of *Little House* were just not the same.

Personally, I thought Mike's perspective was the right one for our show. I believed in his track record: His instincts were pretty right-on. He wanted to be able to veer away from the books when creatively necessary while keeping to the morals and principles so well defined in the original stories. Ed Friendly couldn't see it that way; he had to stick faithfully to those books. By the end of the first season they would part ways for good. Ed would always receive a credit on any shows produced, but he and Mike would no longer act as partners.

I mentioned my frustration with not having much "meat" to work with. "The Raccoon" must have proven me worthy because Mike definitely wrote the episode "The Award" for me. Bill Claxton did a fantastic job directing, and I believe that this was some of the best work I ever did as a child—even if I do say so myself!

At the start of the episode, Miss Beadle announces that the annual scholarship award contest will be held in three weeks. The student who scores the highest on this special examination will win a pristine leather-bound edition of *Webster's Dictionary*. My eyes get so big. I can't imagine anything better than that.

I go home and tell Ma all about it and that I intend to win. She cautions that there are older kids entering the contest, too, who might know more than I do and that maybe I shouldn't get my hopes up.

I reply, "Pa says you can do anything if you set your mind to it. I'll win, you'll see."

I let Miss Beadle know that I've hit a snag in my studying, and she loans me her beautiful American history book to help.

That night, I'm so excited about this prospective award that I can't sleep. I'm sitting at our dresser in our little loft reading when the lamp light wakes Laura. I get back into bed and wait for Laura to fall back to sleep, then I creep out to the barn with Miss Beadle's history book. I light the oil lamp (that was new for me; I'd never lit a match before) and set it on a milking stool next to me in the stall. (Right about here in the episode, is where my son, Griff, about eleven at the time, said as he watched, "Oh. Oh. She shouldn't be doing that." And, "Oh, no. This is not good." Then, "She fell asleep!" I loved the way he kept referring to me as "she." He really got into it.)

In the scene, I am asleep and proceed to knock over the stool with the oil lamp. It ignites the straw in the barn, and a fire breaks out. I awaken, scared to death, and try to right things but only make it worse.

I scream, "Fire! Fire!" and Ma comes running. She sends us girls for water from the creek as she leads the animals out of the barn and beats at the fire with old gunny sacks and the water we bring. She does a remarkable job of putting out the fire. It looks "real"—as though she was running on adrenaline.

I can barely speak through my scared sobbing, but I try to apologize.

Ma screams, "How many times have I told you . . ." And then, "Forget about that examination. You are *not* taking it!"

She, as a mother, can only think of what really *could* have happened to her daughter, and reiterates that to me next morning. I can't talk to her; I just want to try and clean up the mess I've made. As I rake the burned straw in the barn, I find Miss Beadle's book—ruined.

And I thought things were bad before . . .

Caroline regrets losing her temper and confesses to Reverend Alden. She even considers letting this punishment go.

But he says, "Without constancy, a child has no rules to live by."

She agrees and says, "Nor do we."

On our way to school, Laura offers to buy me "a whole penny's worth of licorice" to try to cheer me up, so we stop at the Mercantile where I notice a HELP WANTED sign and inquire to Mr. Oleson about it. Richard Bull portrayed the kindly, henpecked Nels Oleson with great sincerity. He was just as nice off-camera and every scene with him was fun. So Mr. Oleson explains that the job would be every day after school, plus all day Saturdays. The pay is fifty cents a week. And a new copy of that beautiful history book? One dollar. I can finally begin to see the light at the end of this tunnel.

I try to tell Miss Beadle that I cannot take the test, but I can't do it. I cannot tell her as I was supposed to because I don't have the book to give back to her. The day before the big exam, I'll have a *new* history book to give her.

Laura asks, "What if Ma asks if you've told Miss Beadle?"

I reply, "Never cross your bridges 'till you get to them. That's what I'm gonna do. I'm gonna wait for my bridges."

Ma says I can take the job as long as I keep my grades up and do my chores. I am relieved that she says yes.

Shooting in Oleson's Mercantile was fun. Almost everything in the store was real—even the candy. Old and hard, but real all the same. There was a small nook (where I study in this episode) and the storeroom where we occasionally shot with Nels and/or Harriet. You can see the Oleson living room off to the left of the counter, as well.

Miss Beadle comes into the Mercantile and asks me when I have time to study. My lies (or omissions) are beginning to mount up. I tell her that I'm allowed to use the books in the store, and I actually do start to do that.

These Oleson's Mercantile scenes were all shot on the last two days of this episode, which happened to be a Thursday and Friday, as I recall. I was having a great week. I had a terrific episode to shoot, more "meat" than I could have ever imagined, and on top of all this, I was invited to Leslie Landon's birthday. I was so surprised and happy to be invited to that birthday party. I was working so hard on this episode, and I just couldn't believe that I had such a fun event to look forward to as well.

That night, in the episode, I sit at the window in our loft, working by moonlight. I tell Laura that I'm doing my homework now because I used my free time at Oleson's to study for the exam. I explain to her that I tried to do the right thing, but I can't disappoint Miss Beadle. She *wants* me to take the test and thinks I have a good chance of winning. If I *do* take the test and I win, I think Ma will be so proud, she won't be angry.

Laura asks, "What if you don't win and Ma finds out?"

I say, "I'll just *have* to win. I'll just have to."

We have a montage showing how hard I am working: leaving school for the day and walking to my job at the Mercantile. Studying at Oleson's on my down time. Doing my chores at home. Boy, I worked hard! Studying in the loft by moonlight—again. Yawning in class. Reading a book while walking home from work.

Three weeks have passed, and I have earned (a whopping) one dollar and fifty cents. I spend one dollar on the replacement history book to give to Miss Beadle.

It is the day before the big exam, and I quietly thank Miss Beadle for loaning me the book and give it back to her. If she only knew. She misinterprets my heavy heart as nerves and worry about the looming test. I *still* don't tell her.

That evening I give Ma the remaining fifty cents toward fixing the barn. Is that a responsible kid, or what? But Caroline can't believe that's all I was paid for all that work. Again, I omit any explanation and simply say, "I didn't mind" and "It was fun." As I watch this today, I am struck by what white teeth I had. Those Pearl Drops really must have worked. That night, I am up, once again, studying. I remember Bill Claxton telling me, "I need to *see* you thinking, Missy. I need to see it in your eyes." That was hard, but I got it, and I never forgot it. That was a good director's note.

It is finally the day of the examination, and we girls go off to school. Caroline goes to the Mercantile and while there has a "word" with Mr. Oleson as to how difficult it must be to get help at fifty cents for three weeks. He explains to her what really happened and how I spent the rest of my money.

Miss Beadle wants all children who are not taking the exam to go outside. I don't budge. Laura can't believe I'm staying inside with the test-takers. While Ma is in town, she looks for me at school. Laura tells her that I am inside. She looks in and sees me taking the test. She leaves, and she is NOT happy.

All of the children are assembled for Miss Beadle to announce the winner of "The Award." It is Arnold Lundstrohm who accepts that beautiful dictionary to lots of applause. Tears run down my face, and I run out of school.

Later that day, Miss Beadle rides out to our house to show our Ma "exactly what she wanted to see." She tells Caroline that Mary did not take the exam but instead wrote her explanation why. What a great kid, huh?

Caroline goes looking and finds me sitting beneath a huge tree. We take a moment and then run together and embrace. We forgive each other and are best friends again. Watching this, I am reminded of some times that I felt perhaps I'd been too hard on my own daughter, Piper, when she was younger. I can remember some very long school days when I couldn't *wait* for her to finish so I could tell her I was sorry that I'd had to give out whatever punishment it was at the time and how *very* sorry I was that I'd been so harsh. The punishment stayed put; so did our friendship. Just like in this episode. That Landon guy was pretty smart and a pretty good parent, I'd say.

Chapter Seven

Magic Mountain in Disguise

It was late Friday afternoon, and we'd just finished "The Award." Claxton yelled: "Cut! And that's a print!"

He came over and gave me a pat on the shoulder and said, "Good job, Missy, you really worked hard today."

I said, "Thanks, Bill. It was fun. This whole episode has been fun. I'm glad you directed it, Bill. I hope it turns out as good as it feels now."

To which he replied, "Don't worry, kiddo, it's going to be good, and you're going to be happy."

I smiled. He asked me if I had any plans for that weekend.

I quickly launched into, "It's Leslie Landon's birthday and I'm invited. It's a sleepover and we get to go to Magic Mountain tomorrow!"

Bill said, "Have a great time, Missy, and say happy birthday to Leslie for me."

"Sure Bill, and thanks."

I hurried off to my dressing room to lose the pioneer garb and throw on some way cooler 70s clothes. I asked Allan, our makeup man, if he could give me something that would quickly remove makeup, as I didn't have time to go home before the party. Mike Landon had an olive-toned complexion and because he photographed so much darker than the rest of us, they wanted us to blend in with him. We had to wear a shade of makeup that was much deeper and more orangey-tan than our natural choice would be. We couldn't get away with wearing this makeup on the street. It was far too obvious and would attract too much attention. Allan came through with cold cream and Sea Breeze astringent to finish me off, and before I could ask, Larry Germain, our hair stylist, handed me a brush so that I could do a quick once-over. I was ready.

My mother drove me from Paramount to Beverly Hills in about twenty minutes. I was glad it didn't take too long because I was meeting everyone at Ah Fong's Chinese Restaurant, and I wanted to be able to eat with the other kids. I was also excited to go to this restaurant. I loved trying new places and new foods.

I felt a bit shy walking into the restaurant, knowing I was the last to arrive, but Mike and his wife Lynn made me feel comfortable right away. Mike told me he'd seen the dailies (film that is shot each day and screened for the executives the following day) and that everything was looking great. I told him how much I liked his script and that I appreciated the opportunity he had given me.

Shop talk ended, and I went to sit with Leslie, her friends from her school, and Melissa Gilbert, as well. They handed me a little packet that turned out to be "Paper-Wrapped Chicken." Kind of teriyaki and steamed, I think. Yum. Many other delicious appetizers and entrees followed with birthday cake and the obligatory fortune cookies for dessert.

After dinner, we all climbed into a waiting limousine parked out front. These cars were still pretty new to me and terribly exciting to ride in. We drove along North Beverly Drive and over to Tower Road where we wound around and up this beautiful street until we came to the Landon home: a stately English Tudor complete with motorcourt. This home had previously been owned by Bill Cosby, and Mike used to say it was a good thing he was steadily employed, because just buying the toilet paper for eleven bathrooms could put you in the poor house. It had seven bedrooms and many formal living areas as well as a large gourmet kitchen and servant's quarters. There was a grand formal staircase and a small *back* staircase that led from the kitchen directly up to the bedrooms. I know about this because we kids were up and down it making Jiffy Pop popcorn several times during the night. I was impressed that Leslie made it by herself, especially when there were clearly many people around to do things for her. This was a normal family, though. No one behaved as though they were any better than anyone else. Mike and Lynn were good parents, and their kids were exceedingly nice and polite.

We stayed up late watching Leslie and her brother, Mike Jr.'s, favorite scary movies. These two definitely took after their dad. It's just the kind of thing he liked to do: climb on top of the bed, eat popcorn, and watch movies.

The next morning at breakfast, I remember thinking that I'd never seen ornate silver tea sets in a kitchen before. When I saw the rest of the downstairs in the daylight, I noticed there were *more* of them in the other areas of the house. I later came to understand that these were very popular, albeit expensive, gifts, and the tea sets in the kitchen were just there because they'd run out of places to put them.

Mike gave me a tour of the pool area and the *Bonanza* room. Wood-paneled and Western-themed, this room held his leather-bound scripts and many mementos and Western memorabilia. I once gave him a needlepoint picture I made of the Little House and Barn, and he hung it in his Bonanza room.

Mike was a dichotomy. On the set, he *never* carried any money and was always bumming cigarettes. Seeing the opulence in which he lived gave me a much better understanding of his star magnitude. I had never seen this side of his life: no wardrobe, no makeup, just relaxing at home with his family in this perfect setting.

When the tour ended, we all climbed into that limo once again and headed about an hour north of Los Angeles to Six Flags Magic Mountain in Valencia. Mike had asked that Melissa Gilbert and I bring hats and wear clothing that would disguise us a bit so that we wouldn't look so much the way we looked on television and Leslie would be able to enjoy her birthday in relative peace. Because I always wore my hair down on the show, I put it back in a ponytail and pulled my Budweiser bucket hat with fringe down over my forehead. Sunglasses on kids, especially back then, looked really dumb and actually *attracted* attention, so we didn't wear them. Mike did, with a bucket hat pulled down over that famous hair. I can't remember if Melissa did anything with her hair, but she certainly did *not* wear a cap or any other kind of hat or clothing to try to conceal her "Laura-like" appearance. She paraded around Magic Mountain smiling, making direct eye contact with everyone as if to say "Look at me!" Mike was furious. I don't know what she was thinking. I'm sure that it wasn't malicious, but it pretty much foiled any plan we had of going incognito and not being recognized.

Anyone who appears on television at least once a week for years at a time is caught in this dilemma: We want to be good to our fans (they keep us on the air, after all), but we need to be able to try to lead relatively normal lives, as well—*especially* if we have children. This scene at Magic Mountain put Mike in a no-win situation. He and we, to a lesser degree signed autographs and posed for pictures as politely as possible. He tried to explain to the quickly gathering crowd that he was out with his kids, and could they please have some time to themselves? After I signed and posed a bit, I was able to step back to where Leslie, Mike Jr., and the other kids were standing waiting for Mike. The Landon children were used to this, of course, but I couldn't help noticing the sad and resigned expression on Leslie's face. Being the child of a celebrity has its perks, for sure. But it also has *serious* drawbacks. It was at that Magic Mountain moment that I realized what those drawbacks could be. The way I see it, a child should be the center of his or her parents' universe. That child should be dressed up and posed and always the star of the family show. A celebrity's child, whenever they are out in public togehter, always comes second to that famous parent. It is *always* the parent who is the star. I believe this notion upsets the natural balance of things and can be seriously detrimental. Quite a few of these children seem to have grown up relatively unscathed, but there are many others who did not. It's not hard to find articles written about some celebrity's kid in trouble again in any tabloid on any given week. This, combined with the fact that many of these children grow up to follow in their parents' footsteps, only to be *compared*—and usually not favorably— for the rest of their lives with those parents, is the biggest reason I decided to retire when I had *my* kids and to work only occasionally for friends. I never wanted to see that look on my children's faces. And even though it might mean we wouldn't have as much finan- cial freedom—having only one salary—at least they would always have my undivided attention. I have been recognized here and there over the years (people seem to think I look the same—what a com- pliment), but never to the extent that it could be disruptive. I have enjoyed putting my children first and being at home with them day in and day out. As much as I enjoyed my career, I have been even happier playing my parent role. I've worked very hard; it *is* the most difficult job there is and by far the most rewarding.

I'm confident I made the right decision for me and for our family. My beautiful daughter will be a sophomore in college, and my son is happily going into the ninth grade. They are both terrific individuals, and I'm proud to be their mother.

Whenever I am asked when I will return to acting, I explain that in this entertainment business, I can always go back. I've gone from child to ingénue to leading lady, and if I wait much longer, I'll be playing grandmother roles! So, who knows?

In late November 1974, I traveled to New York to ride on a float in the Macy's Thanksgiving Day Parade with Melissa Gilbert and to do publicity for NBC. I was more than happy to do this, as I had always wanted to see what that Big Apple was really like. *Little House* was gaining popularity, and NBC was very high on it. This trip was the first time I noticed how much people seemed to enjoy our show.

We had *lots* of fans. I was treated like a princess while I was there, which made the publicity part much more bearable. I was shy, so doing a lot of interviews and personal appearances definitely did not come naturally to me. I had to learn the appropriate responses to questions that I wasn't used to being asked. Like everything else, though, the more I did these appearances, the better I got, even if it still wasn't my "thing."

After waving and smiling so much that my cheeks were actually sore, I finished the parade and was looking forward to sightseeing and also hoping to do some exploring on my own near my hotel. I was shown a great time by two young NBC executives, Sharon Kovacs and Jeanette Hektoen; I was quite awed by them. I thought they lived such exciting lives in bustling New York City, and I remember very well that one of them wore a perfume that smelled great. They took me to "21," Café des Artistes, and Sardi's, with the framed photos of famous celebrities lining the walls.

I took a long carriage ride through Central Park and toured the Empire State Building. I still love the view from there. I window shopped 'til I dropped. I saw Bonwit Teller, Saks, Bloomies, and Macy's, of course. I splurged off my diet and

I saw *Gypsy* on Broadway, starring Angela Lansbury, with whom I would work ten years later on *Murder She Wrote* at Universal Studios. Angela is a great actress, and it was an honor to work with such a pro and such a kind lady. I played an actress—that was a stretch—who kills her director, played by John Saxon. I remember that John Astin was also in this episode. One day, a very rambunctious kid was bouncing around the makeup trailer. John proudly introduced his son, Sean. All these years later, my son Griffin is totally impressed that I got to meet "Sam" from *The Lord of the Rings*.

tried roasted chestnuts (they smelled better than they tasted) and those great big soft pretzels, which I did like. I also got the "insider version" of the studio tour of NBC at 30 Rock. That was interesting, too. I decided then that New York was a place I could easily live, and I've visited there whenever I can.

I don't live there (yet), but I go often to visit my friend, Pam, who does.

SEASON TWO
May 1975–January 1976

CHAPTER EIGHT

"Four Eyes"

B.W. (Bill) Sandefur was a writer/producer on our show and wrote some great episodes including "Election" and "Four Eyes." The latter was written about his own daughter's experience getting her first pair of glasses. Bill Claxton directed, and this turned out to be one of our most memorable episodes. This was one of those times when *Little House* the television series veered away from *Little House* the book series. In the books, Mary did not need glasses; she contracted scarlet fever and lost her eyesight as a direct result. On the show, the idea of Mary getting glasses proved so much more dramatic and such a "real life" problem to solve that our writers and producers decided to go this route.

My character, Mary, is working harder than ever, even staying after school to complete her work, as demonstrated in the opening scene. Miss Beadle tells me how sorry she is that she has had to give me a report card like none I've ever had before. My work is just not up to its usual high standard.

I say, "Maybe I haven't tried hard enough."

Nellie jumps on this opportunity to tease me and let me know she's happily taking my place as the smartest girl in the class.

After dinner that evening, Pa asks to see our report cards. Laura goes first and shows improvement—although she tries to downplay her achievement so that my report card won't look so bad. Pa looks at mine and is not angry. He says that my work is difficult and that I'll just need to try harder.

Whew! Dodged a bullet, there.

The next morning, I am so unprepared for a test that I pretend to be sick so as not to have to go to school that day. Caroline visits

56

Miss Beadle at school. No one can understand why my grades have slipped. Miss Beadle remarks that I could be left back this year. Caroline is shocked at this news, saying, "That would break Mary's heart."

Miss Beadle, being the solid teacher that she is, wants to do anything she can to help. One day in class, she calls on me to answer a question posed on the chalkboard. I cannot. When we get home from school that afternoon, Laura does my chores for me so that I can spend more time studying.

The lantern light at the kitchen table wakes Charles in the middle of the night. He gets out of bed and, after admonishing me about the late hour, tries to help me with a math problem. Sitting across from me at the table, he scribbles on my slate. He holds it up to show me what I've done wrong and realizes that I cannot see what he's written until I get up and walk over to him. He tests me again, and still I do not see the numbers.

I cry and say, "I can't see them, Pa."

Now that the problem has been identified, steps can be taken to solve it. Dr. Baker confirms the eye problem and sends us to Mankato to see Dr. Burke, who is a specialist there. Pa and I go to see this eye doctor who tells me I have beautiful, healthy eyes and only need a pair of glasses. He tells Charles that sometimes the eyesight deteriorates so gradually that a child may not even notice. He also says that parents are the last to notice and not to feel badly because he did not.

Dr. Burke gives me my glasses and voilà: "I can read anything!" I say enthusiastically.

Dr. Burke explains that it is important I wear these glasses at all times for about a month and, after that, just for school work.

On our wagon ride home, I remark about how beautiful everything is—in such contrast from the trip *to* Mankato.

"I just *love* my glasses," I say.

When we arrive back at the Little House, Ma tells me just what I need to hear—my glasses are so attractive. Laura says I look smart, like Miss Beadle. Charles tells Caroline that I can see twice as well with these glasses.

Back to school I go, after all of the excitement of going to get the new glasses. The first thing Nellie and Willie do is tease me and call me "Four Eyes." Nellie makes a point of saying that she "would never wear the ugly things" to which Laura replies that "Miss Beadle wears glasses and *she's* not ugly."

Nellie retorts, "She doesn't have a husband, either, and Mary's gonna be an old spinster just like Miss Beadle, 'cause no one ever marries a Four Eyes."

The little witch.

I stand to answer a question written on the chalkboard (now that I can *see* the writing on the board) and the kids call me Four Eyes. They are relentless, and those awful words from Nellie keep echoing in my mind: "A spinster, just like Miss Beadle. Just like Miss Beadle."

I ask Ma if she and Pa would have been ashamed if my schoolwork hadn't improved.

Ma says, "Of course not, but you are a fine student, Mary, and you're going to make a fine teacher. Just like Miss Beadle."

Not the words I wanted to hear.

In school the next day, I face even more teasing, and I crack. I just can't take anymore, and I run out of the schoolhouse in tears. I stumble upon an old hollow log and, succumbing to peer pressure, hide the glasses there.

When we arrive home that afternoon, I am questioned as to why I am not wearing my glasses. I lie to everyone and say that I lost them while playing at recess, I guess. I tell them that I took them off for fear of breaking them, put them in my pocket and then, I don't know. They must have fallen out?

Charles is obviously upset and says, "It'll be harvest time before I can get another pair of glasses."

The next morning I tell him that if I don't find my glasses, he doesn't have to buy me another pair. I don't think I should be allowed to have another pair.

Hmmm.

Pa responds, "Lots of people wear glasses, Mary. Even Miss Beadle."

Not again, I think.

I cannot enter the annual history competition because I have lost my glasses. Laura wishes I hadn't, so that I could "beat Nellie real good."

I sit alone in the grass next to the school house when up drives a handsome stranger. He tells me I'm beautiful, hands me a flower, and calls me "Blue Eyes." He has come to see Miss Beadle and I tell him that she is inside.

When I go inside the school, I accidentally interrupt them as they are *kissing*. Miss Beadle formally introduces us; he says he's her beau. The wheels are turning—her *beau*? Girls with glasses *do* get the guys! I ask Miss Beadle if it's too late for me to take the history exam, and as she shakes her head no, I'm outta there! I run back to that old log, retrieve those glasses, and go on to win that history award. Laura is thrilled; I feel guilty. I explain to Pa (what he pretty much already knew) and tell him how sorry I am that I lied. I break down and cry.

He forgives me and says, "Names *do* hurt."

I sniffle and say, "They sure do."

Pa then says that if I keep going this way, I'll be as good a teacher as Miss Beadle.

I affirm, 'That's right, Pa. Just like Miss Beadle."

This episode proved to be important in the lives of many families. I received lots of letters telling me of similar situations kids had gone through and how they had identified with Mary and her struggle. Bill

Sandefur did such a good job with this script, and he helped a lot of people, to boot.

Bill was super talented, quite funny, and *very* loquacious. He generously included me in a family getaway one weekend. Bill and his daughter, Dawn, picked me up early one Saturday morning in his really cool Pantera sports car. We all squished in, and off we went to Big Bear, California, a small ski resort about two hours northeast of Los Angeles. This was my first time skiing, and although I am quite well coordinated and sporty, I must say I was not too comfortable with it. They taught me how to go up the hill on a Platter Pole Lift. I burned one layer of leather off the palms of my gloves but eventually got the hang of it. The chair lifts weren't any easier—oh, that getting on and getting off! I remember that I did a lot of side-stepping up hills, which means I must not have stayed on either apparatus long enough to get to the top.

After a couple of hours and many climbs up the smaller hills, Dawn thought I was ready to advance to medium-sized hills.

"Sure," I said. "Why not?"

Back onto that darned chair lift and up I went, following Dawn. I guess I was supposed to hop off at some point, but she kept on going, so I did too. When we finally reached the top—THE TOP!?!?—I managed to get off. You can imagine Dawn's surprise when she turned and saw me up there with all those *good* skiers.

"Well," she said, "just go from side to side, across the mountain, and go slow. You'll get to the bottom okay."

"Yeah. Okay. Side to side," I muttered, trying to collect myself and my nerve.

I went slowly across the hill. That went all right. I was getting the hang of this. It really wasn't that difficult at all. Then I stepped my way around to go the other way—that was hard. I kept going, but those turns at each side almost killed me. I'd made it about a quarter of the way down. The sun reflecting off the snow was blinding. The wind had kicked up, but I was feeling exhilarated. I tried to turn to the right and both skis decided to face straight *down*, and that's where they (and I) went. I careened down the middle of the hill. I put my arms out to both sides to try and balance. The wind rushed past me. The landscape was a blur. My heart was racing as fast as I was! I didn't stop until I finally hit the bottom, then the flat, and then the fence. Not hard, though. I almost fell, but managed to stay upright. I was breathing hard. I let my pounding heart slow down.

"Whew!" I said. "That was so scary! That was *so* fun!"

And, of course, like with my own kids, just when you start really having fun, it's time to leave. Back we squished into the Pantera, but what a fun day.

EXT. LITTLE HOUSE — NIGHT

CHARLES sits on the tree stump smoking his pipe. CAROLINE appears in the doorway.

                CAROLINE
    Charles. The girls are going to bed.

                CHARLES
    Be right there to tuck them in.

              BILL CLAXTON
         (behind the camera)
    And . . . cut.

Mike and Karen start off the set. Missy ENTERS, moving toward them. BILL SANDEFUR, who'd been standing on the edge of the set, moves forward to Mike and Karen, picking up his story.

                SANDEFUR
    Sooo. She's blowing down that
    mountain, right in the middle. She
    looks like Jesus! Poles out to her

```
CONTINUED:

              SANDEFUR (CON'T)
    sides. She was great! She made it! I
    was worried, though . . .

              MICHAEL LANDON
    You did WHAT? You took her WHERE? She
    went SKIING???!!!

Missy quickly turns right around and ducks back
into her dressing room, not wanting to get into
this!
```

Poor Bill almost lost his job over this. Our insurance doesn't cover these kinds of dangerous or reckless activities. I got a talking-to as well, and you can be sure, I did not ski again while under contract to NBC!

Chapter Nine

"The Campout" and
"Remember Me" Parts 1 & 2

"The Campout" was directed by Bill Claxton and shot mostly on location in Sonora, California. It was a good time for us to get out of smoggy Los Angeles and up into those beautiful Sierra Nevada Mountains.

I had begun to notice a subtle edginess between Mike and Karen. I didn't know exactly what it was about or what had precipitated it, but something about their relationship was definitely different. I wondered if it could be the fact that Karen didn't have as many opportunities to "act" as she might have liked. As the years wore on, she could have placed in the *Guinness Book of Records* for the number of times she said, "More coffee, dear?" and, "Close the door!" She always did a good job with whatever it was she was given—I'm just not sure if she felt appreciated enough.

Crossing Michael Landon was not a good idea. He could make your life miserable if he wanted to. Mike had his own demons and insecurities, many of which are chronicled in his autobiographical television Movie of the Week: *The Loneliest Runner*. Any creative ideas Karen may have had were consistently shot down by Mike. Karen might ask, "What if I got up on my line and moved to the stove?"

Mike would reply tersely, "No. I don't think so."

Karen might say, "I think I should *say* something to defend her, here."

Mike would say, "I think it's fine the way it is," and shut her down completely. It must have been very frustrating for her.

This situation progressively worsened to the point where the two of them only spoke to each other when absolutely necessary. I think Mike was doubly mad because *he* was the one who had fought the network to hire her. Needless to say, the tension on the set was high at these times.

"The Campout" starts with the announcement of a holiday from school and cheers of delight from the kids. We Ingalls girls are happy to be included in Pa's fishing trip and are looking forward to a good time on this family outing. Nellie and Willie think that we will have an unfair advantage collecting the leaves needed for a school project due upon our return to class. These two pester and bug their father until he caves and does what they want. Mr. Oleson drives out to our home one night to try to find out just where our pa is planning to go, so that he can take Nellie and Willie to the same spot and thereby even up the odds.

Charles generously invites the three to come along and join the party. We girls are horrified—two long days with them?

Harriet decides to go along, as well; no way that she's going to let Caroline go without *her*. Now, it's Nels who is horrified. He had hoped for a little break from his nagging wife—no such luck.

Their entire family arrives early on the morning of the trip and only then do we find out that Mrs. Oleson is coming with us. Pa tries to do anything and everything to get out of this trip. As he mutters to himself about how his quiet fishing trip is ruined, Mike lets slip an unthinkable "Wow." That is just one (and one of the worst, I might add) of the *banned* words that were never used back in the 1870s and therefore were not allowed to spring from our lips. That's when it pays to be the boss! Finally he does the *right* thing and decides to make the best of it. It's only two days.

Mrs. O. is actually trying hard to keep up and be a good sport. She does *not* want to be outdone by Caroline. Nellie and Willie stick to us girls "like flypaper," so as not to miss out on any leaves that we might collect. In his greed, Willie picks a bunch of poison ivy he thinks I had wanted.

As I watch this episode, I am struck by how beautiful the scenery is. We hike through the forest with snow-capped mountains in the background and come upon a rushing river. These remote location scenes usually involved only the Ingalls family, and it was different having other cast members with us. My mother and I went out to dinner one evening with Alison Arngrim and her mother, Norma MacMillan. They were used to Hollywood and the "business." Her mother was the voice of "Casper the Friendly Ghost." I thought that was so cool.

The men go fishing as the two women set up their respective tents at the campsite. Mrs. Oleson has a few difficulties but generally has a great attitude and tries hard. All of us kids show off our leaves to our parents. The poison ivy comes out, and Mrs. Oleson doesn't know what it really is. She handles it—a lot. Laura and I notice all of this, but there is nothing we can do about it, so we keep our mouths shut.

The next day, it is obvious that Willie and Mrs. O. have the dreaded "ivy," but both Charles and Caroline are pleasantly surprised at Harriet's good spirits. Nellie, Laura, and I head off to hunt for more leaves. Willie stays behind, scratching. Nellie and Laura go to look near the river. After being warned by Laura, Nellie still gets too close to the edge and slips. Laura tries to help her but falls in, as well. The stunt doubles for Laura and Nellie do not look very credible in these first shots of this scene. They look like adults dressed up and wearing wigs. That's a real problem. It is necessary to use stunt professionals at these times, and they are always adults, but it's *very* hard to make even smallish adults appear to be children. They photograph a bit better as the scene progresses.

The adults have started to worry. Nels and Charles go out looking for the girls, who are now getting close to the falls and risk serious injury. Laura and Nellie are clinging to some tree branches for dear life because Nellie can't swim and Laura won't leave her. They ride along with the ever-strengthening current of the river.

There is shallow water just before the falls and the girls are able to climb onto shore. Naturally, Nasty Nellie blames the whole thing on Laura, who must fight back and stand up for herself, telling Nellie that she didn't need to risk her own life; that she *could* swim and that Nellie should be grateful that Laura saved her life. Melissa Gilbert did a good job in this scene. I really believed her.

Meanwhile, back at camp, Harriet and Ma and Willie and I are . . . bonding.

After their ordeal, once everyone's back at camp, Nellie tells a whopper of a lie, blaming Laura, of course. Mrs. Oleson's true personality reappears, and we are all adversaries ever after.

Once back at school, Nellie and Willie are deemed to have the best leaf collection, but unfortunately Miss Beadle is now the one scratching.

Mike wrote and directed "Remember Me," a two-part episode guest-starring Patricia Neal, who had won a Best Actress Academy Award for *Hud*, also starring Paul Newman. These shows were well written and well acted and stood out as two of our best of Season Two.

Part 1 begins with a mean farmer pulling out a burlap sack, taking three little pups from their mother, and stuffing them into the sack. The mother whines plaintively as she watches the man load the bag containing the pups into the back of his wagon and drive away.

The farmer pulls up to the edge of a pond and begins to place large rocks in the sack with the pups. At that moment, Laura and I are running near the pond. We hear the whimpering puppies and look to see what the man is doing. The man throws the weighted bag into the middle of the pond and drives off. Laura and I are horrified and proceed to dive in to try and rescue the pups. I find the bag in the murky water (of that little lake behind Magic Mountain, once again) and grab hold of it and swim to shore. I begin to pull the pups out, one, then the next, and the next. The bag is not empty, but it's not moving either. Neither Laura nor I want to find a dead puppy, but I get my act together and reach inside.

"Laura, it's a rock. A silly, old rock," I cry in relief.

We keep the three puppies in the barn with our dog, Jack, until we are able to find good homes for them.

Patricia Neal played the widow Julia Sanderson in this episode, and I was very excited to be working with an actress of her caliber. She used a teleprompter while she worked with us, because the stroke she'd suffered somewhat earlier affected her ability to memorize dialogue. It certainly didn't affect her acting ability! She did a wonderful job in this role.

Mrs. Sanderson and her children—John Jr., played by Radames Pera (*Kung Fu*'s young Caine); Carl, played by Brian Part; and little Alicia, played by Kyle Richards—come out to our house for a visit.

The three Sanderson children love the puppies, and Alicia has even named one, "Mine." Her brothers put her up to asking their mother for the pup because she is the youngest. Alicia asks, and her mother says yes, just as her big brothers told her she would. The little girl is thrilled.

Julia goes to see Dr. Baker. Julia has known for a while that she is sick but now feels an urgency she doesn't understand. As it turns out,

Kyle is the youngest sister of the Richards girls. Kathy (Hilton) is the oldest, then Kim, whom I mentioned earlier, and then Kyle. She was absolutely adorable back then, and we all loved to spoil her. I've run into her a couple of times over the years, and we both had children at the same French school in Los Angeles for a time. Kyle and Kim are aunts of Paris Hilton. Their sister, Kathy, is Paris's mother. It's strange to think of Paris Hilton and *Little House* being related in *any* way!

she doesn't have long to live; she could die any time now, the doctor confirms. Her thoughts immediately go to her children. She must provide for them.

Julia goes to see Charles, who is busy plowing her field for her, as he has done since her husband passed away. She tells him her bad news, and he is understandably shocked. Julia tells Charles that she needs help, not sympathy. She needs to find a home for her children.

"Pity wears off pretty quick, and it's a poor substitute for love," she says, emphatically. She doesn't want anyone to take them because they feel sorry for them, and she makes Charles promise to help her children find a home if she dies too soon. The music alone in this scene could make you cry.

That evening, Julia tells her three children what's about to happen. Radames Pera is great as he reacts to this news. He was a fine young actor. Julia will talk to the congregation in church on Sunday, and she wants her kids to hold their heads high and be proud of who they are.

Sunday arrives, and Julia says to her friends and neighbors in church, "I always thought I was too ornery to die, but it seems I was wrong. God must have found some good in me, 'cause he's calling me early." She explains that her children will be needing a family and says, "It takes nine months to have one child, so folks should at least think on it a day or so, before having three."

Our two families, along with Grace Snider, played by Bonnie Bartlett, and Isaiah (Mr. Edwards) have a picnic after church. Julia says, "I want them to remember me laughing."

There is a montage of all of us, except Laura, playing with Mr. Edwards. She is off by herself, and she is scared. She tells Pa she doesn't know what she'd do if anything happened to him or Ma. Pa says, "That's the way you live this life, each day, one at a time."

As Julia gets weaker and is bedridden, she gives Reverend Alden something that she's written to be read at her funeral, and she makes a point of telling the Reverend to please keep it short. He nods and agrees that, "Brevity was never one of my strong points."

She tells him to be sure not to mumble, and he says, "Loud and clear. You'll hear me."

Julia tells Charles that it will be up to him now to make the choice: "Grace will take care of the children until you make your decision."

The funeral takes place in the pouring rain. Reverend Alden delivers the eulogy and reads the short piece that Julia wrote.

When he finishes, he says, to himself,

"Loud and clear."

Early in Part 2, we girls are explaining to Pa that we are having trouble finding a home for the last puppy. Nellie would like to have the pup, but we don't want to give him to her, because we don't think she'll really love him. Pa says that the puppy can stay in the barn with Jack for "As long as it takes. It wouldn't be right to send that pup off to some home he wouldn't be happy in."

What a good dad.

Mr. and Mrs. Anders come out to our home to talk about the Sanderson children. But they are only interested in adopting the two boys, and Charles won't separate them.

"All they have is each other."

After they leave, Caroline says, "He wants farmhands, not children."

Mr. Edwards helps Grace look after the kids. He is still haunted by the loss of his *own* family years before. Hard though he tries to fight it, he has come to love these children.

Charles says, "Four weeks and we're no closer to finding a home for these children than we were when we started."

Caroline tells him, "Mr. Edwards is really spoiling them rotten. They can already spit further than any children in Hero Township!"

Mrs. Oleson's wealthy cousin, Miss Farnsworth, expresses interest in adopting Alicia. Miss Farnsworth would like to have a child and an heir. She thinks that it might work out if the Anders adopted the boys, as they had previously offered. All of the children would be well cared for, and she would be able to give Alicia every advantage.

Charles feels like he has no choice and is thinking of splitting up the children. He wishes he could take them all himself. A picnic is arranged for after church on Sunday so that Miss Farnsworth may spend some time with Alicia and get to know her a bit. As we kids play in the pond, Grace and Isaiah look on in silence.

Miss Farnsworth confronts Isaiah, saying, "You don't like the idea of my adopting her."

He answers, "I just think there's things more important to a child than a big house and lots of money, that's all."

Miss Farnsworth responds, "This may come as a surprise to you, but even rich people can love."

Miss Farnsworth tells Charles that she would most definitely like to adopt Alicia and he says, "Will you love her?"

Charles does not want to divide this family but feels that he must. He talks to the children. Mike was so good in this scene. He is torn up inside, and it comes across beautifully as he says, "I wanted to find a home for you together, but I couldn't."

Radames, as John Jr., says, "Ma told us to do whatever you said. She said you knew best. We know you tried. We'll be alright."

This scene just tears your heart out. Whew!

Nellie Oleson spills the beans about Miss Farnsworth adopting Alicia, and I storm home furious with Pa. He says how sorry he is, and I just break down because I'm so sad.

Laura tells Pa that she is giving the last pup to Nellie because, just like with Alicia, "It doesn't matter if he's happy. Just so he's got a home—*any* home."

Ma talks to Laura and says, "There are a lot of decisions we have to make in this life that we wish we didn't have to. Your pa has made one of those decisions."

The three Sanderson children tell Isaiah and Grace that they will miss them. Grace and Isaiah are morose but can't bring themselves to say what needs to be said. In church on Thanksgiving, little Alicia takes hold of Isaiah's hand and looks up at him as only she can. He melts. As we all prepare to say goodbye to Alicia, Isaiah suddenly says, "I think these children ought to stay together."

He tells Grace that he loves her. He's not afraid to say it anymore, and he loves these kids, too. "If you all will have me, I'll do my best to make you happy."

Back into the church we go, but this time for the long-awaited wedding of our closest friend. After the vows are exchanged, Isaiah picks up Alicia, and the camera freezes on her face as she hugs him. Patricia Neal's voice is heard saying the words her character wrote:

> Remember me with smiles and laughter,
> For that's the way I'll remember you all.
> If you can only remember me with tears,
> Then don't remember me at all.

Oh, Kleenex. Where is that Kleenex?

Chapter Ten

"The Gift" and "Soldier's Return"

"The Gift," directed by Bill Claxton, was a light episode, and we had a bit of comedy to play, which was a departure for us. We kids in the Sunday School take up a collection for Reverend Alden's birthday gift. As treasurer, I am responsible for spending $1.67 on a new Bible and presenting it to him on the big day. We do not tell anyone; this is our class secret. Nellie and Willie steal our idea—ordering the finest Bible they can find to give to him themselves.

At home in our loft that evening, I see a Bible advertised in a catalog for $1.50. But Laura focuses on an expensive one for $3.00. I say no, of course. Laura keeps looking and sees an ad for "Dr. Briskin's Homeopathic Remedies." $1.50 for twelve bottles—which we could sell for a profit.

I let her know in no uncertain terms that, "We can't spend the money for anything but Reverend Alden's birthday Bible."

Laura keeps trying to persuade me to change my mind. She says, "We could make money to buy him the really nice Bible." She uses one of Pa's lines: "You just have faith and work hard and everything'll come out all right."

I finally give in.

Our order arrives in the post, and I say, "There sure are a *lot* of them." And each one is labeled with the different maladies they're sure to cure.

But, off I go to sell medicine for toothache and earache, for twenty-five cents each.

I go to see "Mrs. Foster," whose real name was actually Ruth Foster and who was also Karen's stand-in. It was said that it was her home that was used (and I believe there may have been money involved) for Mike to conduct his affair with *my* stand-in, Cindy, which would take place a few years later.

Anyway, Mrs. Foster doesn't buy. Strike one.

Laura goes to the Hobson Pig Farm to try to sell the medicine. An adorable little boy grabs one bottle of our pills and feeds it to the pigs. Strike two. And we're out twenty-five cents. When we meet up at the end of the day, we are depressed. Our business venture isn't working out so well. A sad wanderer drives up to our home, selling Indian medicine jewelry and telling tall tales. He manages to get himself invited in for dinner, offering Ma twenty-five cents. She won't take the money, of course, so he trades her one of his necklaces. None of this gets past us; we quickly learn the art of the swindle.

Pa says, "People buy better if you tell them a sad story."

Laura decides she'll try selling before school and starts telling lies about her Ma and Pa's rheumatism. She says, "Pa uses Dr. Briskin's, and it's the onliest thing that helps him." And, "We're selling to put food on the table."

An old lady wants the medicine, but can't afford it, has no one, boo hoo hoo. Laura gives her the medicine for free. It's all about the alcohol—the old lady wants to get sloshed.

When I hear this news, I yell, "What do you mean you *gave* it to her?" I continue with despair.

"We're never gonna sell anything. Never!"

Strike three, and now we're out fifty cents.

I am getting desperate. After school, I quiz Miss Beadle as to her health and tell her to *please* let me know if she gets to "feelin' poorly."

Strike four. Can you tell I'm not a baseball aficionado?

Laura dresses in an old gunnysack with no shoes and a very dirty face. She pretends to be motherless and poor. As it happens, the woman she tries to scam has just seen our Ma in town, and Laura is caught in her lies.

Strike five; we're out.

We are really screwed. Even if we had sold every bottle, we still couldn't have ordered the Bible and gotten it in time for Reverend Alden's birthday. We decide to pick out some exotic sickness from the labeling on what's left of our medicine collection and be sick on that day.

We've contracted laryngitis but tell Pa we're sure we'll get our strength back in a few hours—conveniently *after* church.

Pa lets us have it. "Laryngitis means you can't talk," he says. "Now, spill it."

We do, and Pa says that we'll have to go to church and tell the Reverend the truth.

Laura and I go into the church and confess. Reverend Alden asks to keep the wooden box. As he gives his sermon, he tells the congregation that, "When you're a minister, everyone gives you a Bible."

Hearing that, Nellie tries to hide the very expensive Bible that she and Willie purchased for him. Reverend Alden goes on to say how the Sunday School children have given him a case in which to keep safe his special old Bible, given to him by his father.

He says, "It's the gift of love that's the greatest gift of all."

One day while we were shooting interiors at Paramount, Mike pulled me aside.

"Hey, Missy . . ." he said.

I answered, "Yeah, Mike?"

"I'm sure you've been hearing about the movie I'm going to shoot soon, *The Loneliest Runner*?"

"Yes, I have, Mike. Is it really all about your life growing up?"

"Yes it is, Miss, except that I was a javelin thrower in New Jersey, instead of a marathon runner in California."

That explains those huge shoulders and arms, I thought.

"That's so it will be easier to shoot on the streets of L.A., right?" I asked.

"Good thinking, Missy, and you're right about that. It can be hard to shoot in neighborhoods here in L.A. that *don't* have palm trees lining the streets. It's also better storytelling to make me a runner. You'll see when you read the script."

I looked at him quizzically. Why would I get to read the script? I thought.

Mike said, "You look so much like Nancy Rizzi, my first girlfriend, and I was wondering if you would like to play her in the movie?"

I couldn't believe what I was hearing.

"Do you want me to audition for you, Mike?" I asked.

"No, of course not, Missy. I am *offering* you this role. I already know you can do the job," he answered.

Wow. Wow. Wow! I can't believe this is happening, I thought. No audition, even. Unbelievable!

"So, you'll need to read the script and let me know if you'd like to sign on, okay?" he asked.

"Yes, absolutely, Mike, I will. I'm sure I will love it, and *thank* you for asking me, really," I answered gratefully.

Mike replied, "No problem, kiddo. Like I said, you're perfect for this part."

That was a great day. I read the script for *The Loneliest Runner* and loved it and my character, Nancy. We would take a three week hiatus, or break, from *Little House* in the fall of 1976 in order to shoot this TV movie in time for an air date of December 20, 1976.

After many years away, Mrs. Whipple's son moves back to Walnut Grove in "Soldier's Return," written by Bill Sandefur and directed by Bill Claxton. Richard Mulligan, probably best known for his work on the late-night comedy *Soap*, guest-starred as Granville Whipple and gave a good performance as a struggling war veteran. For me, this episode was very dark; almost scary. I remember attributing the drug abuse more to the war than to the pain from the injury. I guess it was the upsetting images of the war that gave me this wrong impression. It's a tragedy when you think that his addiction was originally started by a doctor's ill-conceived prescription. And, God knows, war itself can wreak havoc on a person's soul.

Granville is riding along in his wagon when he spots us girls and asks for directions to Mrs. Whipple's place. I introduce myself and Laura, telling him that I work for his mother as a seamstress. She's going to be so happy to have her son home.

Granville is a decorated war hero from the battle of Shiloh twelve years earlier. He suffered a bad leg injury and developed an addiction to the morphine that was prescribed for his pain. His mother finds a small amount of the drug in a tin box beside his medal for heroism. Seeing her worried look, he tells her that he's been clean now for nine months.

"I just keep enough around that I know it's there. I won't shame you with it, Ma. Otherwise I would never have come home."

His ma says, "The doctor himself said you couldn't help it if you craved it."

To which Granville asserts, "Ma, I don't need it anymore."

At home that night, I tell the family about meeting Mr. Whipple, his medal, and the fact that he even received a letter from General Grant. I explain that he was hospitalized for a long time in Philadelphia, which is where he has been living since the war. He is a fine musician and plays many instruments. He played in an orchestra there and taught music, as well.

I ask Pa if he was ever in a war.

"No, Mary, and I pray to God I never have to."

Laura says, "I bet you'd be a hero and win a medal."

To which Pa responds, "Half-Pint, I think most men would trade any medal to forget the memory of war."

At the Whipple's house, Granville is trying to acclimate. He stares at his old bugle that he played in the war, which his mother has kept all of these years. It haunts him. He still experiences flashbacks of Shiloh and tries hard to shut them out. He nervously goes to the small tin and picks up the packet of morphine and his medal. He puts the morphine back; resists temptation.

Granville lies down, still holding the medal. He is remembering the war. The dream sequences in this episode all take place in a forest at night. We *never* shot "night for night" on *Little House*. That is to say, we didn't use the real night sky. We shot "day for night," which means carefully shooting outside in daylight, but making it look like night, using special filters on the camera and dialing the light level down in the film lab. It never looks as good as the real thing.

Mrs. Whipple takes her son to Oleson's Mercantile to meet Mrs. Oleson and talk to her about advertising the music lessons Granville would like to give. Mrs. O. is happy to help bring culture to Walnut Grove and would like Nellie and Willie to become his first students.

A few days later, Nellie is finishing her flute lesson at the Whipple house. She runs into me there and asks if I am taking music lessons, too.

"No, I'm doing some sewing for Mrs. Whipple," I reply.

Nellie doesn't miss an opportunity to make me feel inferior as she tells me, "My mother thinks music is more important."

Granville can see that my feelings are hurt and that I would also love to be able to afford music lessons. He nicely offers me a deal: If I copy some sheet music for him, he will give me music lessons. I am excited at the prospect at learning to play the piano and happy to perfect my sight-reading as I copy all of those musical notes.

Caroline has invited the Whipples over for dinner. Pa and Mr. Whipple have a banjo/fiddle off and, not surprisingly, Granville wins. He tells Charles that I have been such a help getting his business started and what a good worker I am.

Pa says, "That's my Mary."

Granville says, "Funny, you know, when I left, wasn't much here. Just a few farms. Army looked real good. I spent the last dozen years looking for what was here all the time. People you care about. Folk who care about you."

On a trip to town, Mrs. Whipple and Granville are approached by an old friend that he would rather not have run into. It is the widow of his best friend from the war and her son, Roy Jr., who never got to meet his father. Roy Jr. tells Mr. Whipple that in his father's letters, he wrote that Granville was the "best bugler in the whole blamed army" and asks if Granville could teach him to play, too. He would love to hear about his father from someone who was with him.

Granville looks stricken and tells the boy that the bugle is not a sound he likes to hear anymore. He can't take this. He can't face this boy who looks so much like his best friend. He has to get away. He goes home.

Succumbing to the pressure, he uses his morphine. Now, he must have *more*.

I come to show him the music I've copied, but his personality has changed. He looks at my work perfunctorily and pronounces it unworthy. He rants on and on at me: "You should have done them right the first time. You've not only wasted time, you've wasted paper."

He storms out of the house.

Granville goes to the Mercantile looking for morphine. Mr. Oleson doesn't stock heavy-duty painkillers, ever since Dr. Baker asked him not to, saying, "Folks that use that stuff are liable to hurt themselves worse than what was paining them in the first place."

He exits quickly to go see Dr. Baker.

Before he can get that far, Roy Jr., his army mate's son, runs up to show him his late father's bugle. Granville goes off on him, scaring the poor kid to death.

Dr. Baker examines his leg and says, "That's a long time for it to be causing you pain." He gives Granville something non-addictive;

he knows the signs. The doctor looks at Granville's shaking hand and says, "The only way you'll stop that trembling for good is to fight it through—without morphine."

Granville retorts, "You don't care. You doctors cause it, and you don't care."

He won't let Dr. Baker help him. He's outta there.

I talk to Pa about Mr. Whipple. He explains that Mr. Whipple has experienced much sadness in his life and that we need to be patient with him.

That night Granville breaks into Dr. Baker's office and steals morphine. *All* of it.

Next we find him in his bed, fully clothed. He is hallucinating about the war. In his drugged state, he imagines a dying soldier grabbing him by the collar, but Granville shakes him off and runs away. He suddenly awakens—startled, then goes back into his weird sleep again. When his mother brings his coffee in the morning, she sees that he still has his shoes on, then notices the empty packets of drugs on the bedside table. She takes his stash and leaves the bedroom. She removes her son's medal from the box and places it on the mantlepiece. Just as she is about to throw the rest of the drugs into the fire, Granville pleads, "Mama, don't. Please. I need it, Ma."

Poor Mrs. Whipple can only say, "I don't know where to find the blame. You were doing so well."

Granville says, "I didn't earn this medal, Ma. I'm no hero. I never was. I was just the only one left alive. I'm alive because I ran. I ran and I hid 'til it was all over. Like a coward. Cowardice, Ma. That's punishable by death. There's no medals and no bugles."

His ma says, quietly, "Everyone is afraid sometime. The only way to stop running from a shame is to face it. There's no shame in the truth.

She pleads: "I want my son *whole* again."

Granville interprets her speech to mean that he must go and tell Roy Jr. the truth about what happened and says, "I love you, Ma."

He kisses his mother and leaves.

This is not going to end well.

He has been gone for hours.

Charles and Mrs. Whipple go to look for her son. Charles finds him lying under leaves and branches—hiding just the way he did on that fateful day at Shiloh. Only this time, he does not get up and walk out. He has overdosed.

Reverend Alden, speaking at the memorial service says, "As the bugler asks, this soldier has come home."

Roy Jr. plays the bugle as the screen slowly fades to black.

On my hiatus in the early spring of 1976, I was invited to be part of an "Appealathon" (telethon), set to take place in Perth, Australia. I was happy to go, as was my mother. How often does one have the chance to go to Australia?

The flight from Los Angeles was incredibly long, and as I recall, we made a refueling stop in New Zealand before landing in Sydney. New Zealand looked just as green as you'd expect from the window of that airplane. And Sydney was just a stop—not our destination. We had to fly *another* five hours before we would arrive in Perth. I didn't realize just how much area the continent of Australia takes up: it's like flying from the East Coast to the West Coast of the United States, flying from Sydney to Perth.

In 1976, Perth was an up-and-coming city. It was lovely and spread out, with a lot of new construction going on. My mother and I stayed at a luxury hotel and sampled Kobe beef for the first time there. Delicious!

I worked at the Appealathon—doing interviews, asking for donations, answering telephones, and I met some very talented Aussie actors and actresses. I received a guided tour of the Outback and saw all creatures Australian. The kangaroos were bigger and much stronger than I had expected, and those cute koalas are just that. I talked with some Aboriginal people—even attempting to play the "didgeridoo" that was given to me as a gift.

It was a fascinating trip, well worth the long flights. On the way home, I was relieved to find out that we'd get back that day we had lost while traveling once we crossed the International Date Line!

That was my first and only experience flying on Quantas Airlines. They were great, and as described in the movie *Rain Man*, they have the best safety record around. I am reminded of this because my son, Griff, does a mean impression of Dustin Hoffman saying, "Quantas. Quantas never crashed."

SEASON THREE
May 1976–February 1977

CHAPTER ELEVEN

"The Collection" and
The Loneliest Runner

Johnny and June Carter Cash guest-starred in "The Collection," written by Arthur Heinemann and directed by Mike Landon. Getting these mega–country stars to act in one of our episodes was a real coup—and our set was buzzing with anticipation. What would they be like? Would they be traveling with an entourage? Would they ask for any special treatment? Perks?

As with other recording artists I've met over the years, the Cash family (their young son, John Carter, was an extra in this episode) was down to earth and nice to everyone they came in contact with. I've had the pleasure of meeting Dolly Parton—over the phone— and she is a delight! And I've met Neil Diamond, another super talent who is just as nice and charming as can be.

Singers are almost always excellent actors, as well. This was definitely the case with June and Johnny (we all called him "John"). I remember being so surprised at how good June was portraying Mattie Hodgekiss, the "stand-by-her-man" grifter, with a heart of gold, alongside John's con man, Caleb. She did a terrific job, as did John, and I was beyond excited to work with him as I was featured in this episode and had almost every scene with him.

"The Collection" opens with a wide shot of the vast countryside with a wagon out of control and horses galloping increasingly fast across the screen. We come to realize that it is a runaway, just as Johnny Cash, on horseback, takes notice as well. He rides fast, catches up to the horses, and manages to stop the wagon. He sees a man lying inside, unconscious. We, as the audience, know immediately that this man is our Reverend Alden, but Johnny Cash, as Caleb Hodgekiss, does not. He takes the Reverend back to the little shack that he shares with his wife, Mattie.

Caleb goes through all of the Reverend's things as Mattie tends to the Reverend's fever. He counts his money: one dollar and eighty-seven cents. And he takes special interest in the gold pocket watch inscribed to the Reverend from his congregation in Walnut Grove. Caleb and Mattie learn from his ash-covered clothing that our poor Reverend Alden has been "mighty close to a fire."

When the Reverend finally comes to, Caleb says, "We had to wrastle the Death Angel all night long for you."

Reverend Alden weakly explains that a prairie fire burned out Grey's Corners. The wheat crop and farm houses are all gone. Farmers are living in the church and the livery stable. He was planning on collecting donations in Walnut Grove to help. Since Reverend Alden is in no condition to go, Caleb offers to go himself—to let the elders of the church know about the fire and to do the collecting that needs to be done.

Out in the barn, Caleb is re-born as he dresses in the Reverend's clothing and becomes "Brother" Hodgekiss. He tells Mattie, the Lord meant for folks to be kind and generous: "And *I'm* the one they're gonna be kind and generous to."

Mattie says, "Caleb, you're gonna get in trouble, and this time they won't let you go."

Next, we hear John's voice singing as we see me walking down the road. As the voice grows nearer, I turn to see a man of the cloth approaching on horseback. Brother Hodgekiss rides up and says, "I thought I had ridden through the pearly gates and seen an angel."

I smile and then ask, "Are you a friend of Reverend Alden?"

He answers, "Oh yes, I am. He's a fine man. You might say we're both cut from the same cloth."

What a card. Ha ha.

He asks me for directions to the Ingalls's home, and I of course introduce myself and offer to show him the way. He gives me a ride on his horse (it's still cool to think that I once rode a horse with Johnny Cash!), and off we go to the Little House.

Caleb, a.k.a. Brother Hodgekiss, lies when he tells Charles that Reverend Alden is on his way to Mankato to do what he can with the collecting. Brother Hodgekiss produces a list of people he is to visit while in Walnut Grove, and Charles says that he and Edwards can go to the outlying farms to help. I ask if I can help, too. I can help root out the stingy from the generous. Ma gives me the okay.

I goad the stingy folks into giving more. Mr. Sprague, our town banker, gives an extra ten dollars. I tell Brother Hodgekiss that the Olesons will outdo Mr. Sprague, and after I make the introductions at Oleson's Mercantile, I grab Mrs. Oleson and take her aside into their storeroom. I explain that we are going to need a place to store the things we collect: food, clothing, money. Perhaps she could rent this storage room for, say, fifty dollars?

I add, "We could enter that fifty dollars in the ledger as your donation, and people would be *terribly* impressed."

Mrs. O., looking at the ledger, says, "Mr. Sprague is only giving thirty dollars?"

I reply, "He's temporarily strapped for funds."

I convince Mrs. Oleson to contribute twice as much—sixty dollars!

Brother Hodgekiss has done a good job ingratiating himself into the community. Dr. Baker brings him along on a medical visit to an elderly patient, Addie, who has lost her will to live because she misses her husband. Caleb listens to her, and the two find that Brother Hodgekiss and her late husband are quite a bit alike. They've both been to sea, and they've both been to jail!

Dr. Baker and Addie's dear friend, Mrs. Whipple, are waiting outside on the porch when all of a sudden, singing can be heard coming from the bedroom.

When Brother Hodgekiss emerges from the house, Dr. Baker says, "There wasn't a soul in town that could rouse her. She was dyin' and she *wanted* to die. The Lord must be speaking through you, Brother."

And he adds: "God bless you."

Back at the Hodgekiss home, Mattie is feeling guilty as she tends to Reverend Alden. He says, "You know, in God's eyes you saved my life. I don't know how to thank you."

Mattie spins around and says, harshly, "Well, then don't! I don't *need* your thanks." She is at her breaking point and can't take the kind words from this "mark."

Meanwhile, Mr. Oleson has come to trust Brother Hodgekiss absolutely. He shows him where the extra cash is kept in the storage room, explaining that he keeps it locked at night. He even gives Brother Hodgekiss a key. Caleb is planning to leave Walnut Grove on Saturday with all of the goods and cash he's collected for the homeless of Grey's Corners, but we convince him to stay to give the sermon in church on Sunday.

I say, "People give more on Sunday."

As we drive around collecting donations, I say, "The ones who don't have much—they give the most." I go on, "I bet I know why, because they know what it means to need and not to have."

Brother Hodgekiss replies, "Mary, you know if this suit fit you, I'd let you wear it."

"I declare, you're different from any preacher I ever knew."

"Yeah, I suppose I am," he replies.

We are visiting the Edwards place, and Isaiah asks Brother Hodgekiss to say a few words to comfort Alicia, because her pup has died. She is afraid because she thinks that dogs don't go to heaven.

Brother Hodgekiss begins to tell her a story: There was a whole bunch of rain and *Jonah* builds a big boat. She questions this; he says he just wanted to make sure she remembered her Bible.

As for that big boat, er Ark, he says, "I betcha there were dogs on there, too."

Alicia perks up a little at this.

"You can just be sure He would want a pretty little puppy like yours with Him in heaven."

Alicia asks, somewhat relieved, "Then I'll see 'Mine' again?"

"Sure will," he says.

As Brother Hodgekiss is about to leave, Isaiah stops him and says, "God bless you."

Back at the Hodgekiss home, Reverend Alden is up and about and searching through his things. Clothing is missing from his bag. When he questions Mattie, she says, "You'll get 'em back. I promise ya."

She continues lying, saying, "Folks'll be more generous to a man of the cloth. They give more. You know for yourself they do. It impresses 'em."

"I suppose he's impressing them with my watch?" Reverend Alden asks sarcastically.

"He's takin' for the needy. Lord knows we're needy."

Mattie tells the reverend that if he can just wait for Caleb to return, he can have his things back. "Only don't turn him in, Reverend," she pleads. "Please don't turn him in."

As Caleb uses his key to let himself into Olesons' storage room on Saturday night, Mr. Oleson sees him. Caleb explains that he was checking that everything's locked up tight, and Oleson thanks him for everything he's done to bring our little town together.

Brother Hodgekiss replies, "I didn't do anything." On the way out, he notices the Olesons' pregnant hound dog and asks that Nels give Alicia one of the pups when the time comes. Our town spirit must be rubbing off on him.

It's Sunday morning, and Pa and I are helping Brother Hodgekiss pack up his wagon. He takes off his jacket and vest; I hang them up for him and find the Reverend Alden's gold pocket watch. I put two and two together. No dummy, me. I stare at Brother Hodgekiss, seething! If looks could kill . . .

He finishes packing the wagon and starts to get dressed once again. He notices that the watch is missing, and I say, "It fell out of your pocket."

Brother Hodgekiss, or whoever he is, lies, saying that Reverend Alden lent it to him to make sure he gets to Grey's Corners on time.

I'm not buying it.

John gives a great performance playing this shifty-eyed liar.

Caleb steps into the church; he takes a breath. Watching it, you half expect him to turn around and run the other way. But he doesn't. He continues in. Just then, Miss Addie, on the arm of Mrs. Whipple, arrives in the church to the great amazement of the congregation.

She says, "I got my sass back. God bless you, Brother Hodgekiss."

Please, not again. How many blessings can one guy take? The guilt has gotten to him. And I stare him down. He says, "I can't do what I came here prepared to do today. I can't give you the sermon that I wrote."

He comes down from the pulpit and says, "I've seen people that had little give—because others had less."

Charles says, "You gave too, Brother."

Looking at me, Brother Hodgekiss says, "I took."

He says he wants the congregation to be responsible for taking the contributions to Grey's Corners, just as Reverend Alden comes through the doors and into the church.

Stretching the truth, Reverend Alden says, "I've known Brother Hodgekiss, here, for . . . awhile, and I can tell you out of personal knowledge of the man, that he's given more than any of you realize."

They shake hands and Caleb palms the watch back to the Reverend. He thanks teary me for (presumably) turning him straight.

I loved this episode. I've always loved stories about grifters and con men and being able to be part of one was especially fun. John gave all of the cast and our entire crew and staff personally signed copies of his book, *Man in Black*. And June did something really special for a thirteen-year-old girl: She gave me my very first bottle of perfume. It was Worth, and I'll always remember that.

The only complaint I had about shooting *The Loneliest Runner* was the era in which it was set. I really didn't like fifties clothing; I didn't find them flattering at all. Even worse were the silly sponge curlers I wore to sleep each night so as to achieve that special "fifties" look the next day. Too much primping for me. But everything else about this shoot was fun and exciting. I enjoyed playing a different character. I got to meet Brian Keith, who played Mike's father. Brian Keith! From *Family Affair*, which I used to watch in re-runs after school. Neat! And Mike chose Lance Kerwin to portray him as a boy.

Lance was a terrific young actor. He had done a great job in the third episode of our first season on *Little House*: "The 100 Mile Walk." It was a "buddy" episode, very much the "Western," and it centered around Mike and the men he met out on the road while looking for work. Lance played the son of one of those men that must be told (by Mike, of course) that his beloved

From about the time *The Loneliest Runner* aired in late 1976, for several years, whenever a producer needed teenagers to play a cute couple, they asked for Lance and me. We would go on to shoot the pilot for his series, *James at 15*, and even as late as 1981, we worked together in *Advice to the Lovelorn* with Cloris Leachman. We were good old friends and it was always a pleasure to see him again.

Pa is dead. His work so impressed Mike that when the time came, he knew whom to cast as the lead in his television movie.

The Lonliest Runner begins with Mike (as the adult John Curtis) running into frame and around a huge track to cheers and applause from the crowd. He has won the grueling twenty-six-mile marathon for the United States. As he runs, in a closer angle of the crowd, I can pick out practically our entire sound editing department in the front row. Included are Vince Gutierrez, sound editor, his wife, Linda, and others who worked in looping and Foley (the art of making sound effects to put to picture, such as footsteps, etc.).

Watching grown men and women doing Foley is quite an amusing sight. The film is on a large screen in front of them, and after careful planning and rehearsals, they proceed to record these necessary sounds and noises. One would think that the original footsteps made by the actor would suffice, but no, those footsteps are not loud enough and therefore must be replaced on a recording stage. Depending on the weight of the gait (seriously) the Foley artist might wear heavy boots and maybe even carry weighted bags to be more lumbering, if required. They do all kinds of interesting and silly things in this job. They have long, low boxes of sand and dirt to walk on. Grown men and women run and jump in place to create the effect some kids running and playing. These folks are *very* imaginative and seem to have a great deal of fun at this job.

In the following scene, Mike is doing a pre-interview with the decathlon gold medalist, Rafer Johnson, who is letting him know what kinds of questions he will be asking. For example: "What got you interested in running, John?"

As Mike's character, John, ponders this question, the movie goes back in time to when he was just a thirteen-year-old boy. His alarm clock ringing, Lance Kerwin, as the young John Curtis, jumps up to quickly change the wet sheets on his bed and put on clean pajamas. He puts the soiled laundry into a gym bag in his closet and jumps back into his bed to wait for his father to come in later to wake him.

John Curtis, at thirteen, still wets the bed. His mother does nothing to help him and actually believes that he does it on purpose. She is a dreadful woman who has left poor John in a toddler bed because of his condition. This poor kid is wound so tight you keep expecting him to explode, but he keeps everything inside. He can't go to any sleepovers with his friends; he can't even have his friends up to his bedroom because of that humiliating little bed.

His father is nice, soft-spoken, and unfortunately under his awful wife's thumb. He has made a deal with his wife and his son that if John can stay dry for several nights in a row, he will buy John the nicest, biggest bed he can find. His mother doesn't think it will ever happen.

John starts lying about the bed-wetting partly to get that big bed and also because he just can't take the constant humiliation from his mother. He lies and says that he has football practice every day before school just so he can use most of his lunch money to literally run his laundry to the laundromat. He is often late to school and can't afford much to eat at lunchtime, which is where John and my character, Nancy Rizzi, meet for the first time. We hit it off, and John actually seems happy for a time.

Lance and I had fun working together. We had a lot in common. We were both very serious and perfectionists about our work. We had the same, nice Mrs. Minniear from *Little House* as our teacher, and the same old tables and chairs in our school trailer. Mrs. Minniear asked our props department to *please* cover the old, scarred wooden table tops with . . . something. They did, with heavy white cardboard fastened all around with gaffer's (duct) tape. Just like new.

When I went back to work on *Little House* a few weeks later, that table must have been re-arranged, because I was now sitting where Lance must have been seated during *Runner*. He had written on the white top: "Lance loves Missy, but Missy doesn't love Lance". Awww.

I felt bad. Embarrassed and bad. It never seemed to affect our future relationship, though.

In the movie, there are scenes with his family watching television. His mother is glued to the screen. She alternately ignores and berates John, especially if he dares to interrupt while she's watching one of her shows.

It is a Saturday morning, but John's alarm goes off extra early, as usual. He runs with his gym bag to the laundromat and discovers, to his horror, that it is closed. It must not open as early on the weekend. John is forced to try to hide the bag in the back of his closet until he can try the laundromat again.

That afternoon, John is the hero of the school's football game. He is ecstatic as he rides home with his dad and some friends. As they turn into the driveway, John sees his little bed sheet hanging out from his bedroom window. Right in the front of the house, on the second floor, for the whole world to see. And they do. His mother is despicable. She has achieved her goal: John is beyond mortified.

John quits football because now he must run, and I do mean *run* home from school each day to get his sheet from his window and wash it before any of his friends come home from school and see it. He can't get back to school in time for practice, so football has to go.

While taking gym class at school, John runs around the track. He is *way* ahead of the pack. The coaches take notice and offer to let him run with the varsity team. He's too young to actually be on the team, but he can train with them—he's *that* good.

That evening at dinner, he broaches this idea with his parents. He asks them if he can come home to wash his sheet and then go back to school in time for practice. He'll have just enough time to do it. His miserable mother says that the sheet will wait for him to finish his track practice. He will *not* be allowed to run home first and then go back to school. Another hope dashed. John does not attend practices.

As if that isn't enough, his witch of a mother accepts a sleepover invitation on his behalf. She wants to prove her point that he does this on purpose. If he doesn't wet the bed there, then she'll be proven right and will expect him to be dry at home, as well.

John sits at the window of his friend's room all night to keep himself awake. Morning comes, and all is well, but he is exhausted. Naturally, he cannot keep staying up all night every night, so he continues wetting the bed at home.

One afternoon, as school is letting out, John sees my character's father waiting to drive me home in his beautiful new convertible. He offers John a ride, but he politely declines and runs off in sheer panic. He just *can't* let me see his sheet hanging from that window. He just can't. John runs faster than he's ever run before. His life literally depends on it. On some bends in the country road, he is able to see our car winding along just below. He takes shortcuts wherever possible, trying desperately to outrun that car. Finally he comes to his street and just as he is about to turn, my father's car turns and passes him. The look on Lance Kerwin's face is one of unimaginable defeat. His life is over. He turns and runs away.

He ends up spending the night inside a darkened department store. He seems oddly at ease in the absolute quiet of the store. Understandable—considering the chaos and misery of his life. John makes his way to the furniture section of the store and stares wide-eyed at the beautiful big mattresses there. He picks one and lies down to sleep.

His parents have alerted the police, who call the next morning saying that they've found John, safe and sound, and there will be no charges filed against him. His parents rush to the department store where John tells his father that he was dry last night. He looked at those big beds and *knew* that he would be. His father then confesses that he, too, had been a bed-wetter.

John consoles his father saying, "Oh, I know, Dad, I understand."

What a poignant moment. The child becomes the parent and finally is free to *be* a child. To enjoy his life. The way it should be.

John starts practicing with the varsity team and runs into me, as Nancy. He makes a date with me.

Back at the beginning of the film, with Mike playing John as an adult being interviewed by Rafer Johnson, he has come up with an answer to that question: "What got you interested in running?"

John replies, "I owe it to my mom and dad."

Well, that's one way of putting it.

I've said that Mike was insecure. Perhaps *The Loneliest Runner* explains why. He was born Eugene Orowitz and had every intention of changing his name to Michael *London* until the guy in line ahead of him picked that one. Seriously! So he chose *Landon* instead. He grew up in an environment fraught with anxiety and cruelty. He told me that his mother used to put her head in the oven when she wanted attention. I suppose she wanted to "end it all" with the gas? Perhaps she was a frustrated actress? She certainly was a real drama queen.

Mike was a great father from everything that I saw. But at work, he *was* controlling, and he could also be mean at times. He would single out certain people and tease them publicly and relentlessly. There was a man, Bob, who worked by the camera, loading film and pulling focus for the camera operator. He had a bad stutter, and Mike made fun of him time and time again—and expected all of us to find it funny and laugh. It *wasn't* funny; I didn't laugh. I directly attribute this behavior to the way he grew up. I certainly don't think anyone comes out of a childhood like that unscathed and without serious trauma to the psyche.

There was a good reason that Bill Claxton was my favorite *Little House* director. He collaborated. He really listened to our ideas. He made us feel that no matter what our age, our opinions were valuable. You had to catch Mike on a very good day to get him to change any of his pre-planned blocking of a scene. He would tell our stand-ins where we would be, and where we might move in the scene. The set would then be turned over to the cinematographer and the gaffer (the technician responsible for lighting the set) and "lit" using our stand-ins. The problem with this method is that when we actors arrive on the set, we *occasionally* want to sit down in the scene, not stand. Walk over there, not here, etc., etc. The way Mike directed, we never had much choice. Very, very rarely could you win a creative argument with him. It wasn't only Karen who had problems with Mike—hers were just more significant.

Mike chewed his fingernails down to the quick. He smoked a lot, and he drank a lot, although I can't remember ever seeing him any more than tipsy. He could also be vindictive. I remember him telling me that the main reason he decided to blow up the town of Walnut Grove at the end of *Little House* was so that no one else would ever be able to use our sets.

Having said all of this, I must also say that he was just like the rest of us—flawed. He was a huge television star with huge insecurities, and underneath it all, a huge heart. Mike Landon, the regular guy, was great. I loved him. He looked out for me as I was growing up; stood up for me when a tabloid would threaten to write some hurtful lie. He was always there with a shoulder to lean on, if I needed one. I could always go to him for advice, and I did on more than one occasion. I remember all the times I saw him scribbling away on his yellow legal pad. That's how he wrote all of his screenplays, in longhand—like me, writing this book. I often think of what it would be like if he were alive today. The business has changed so much. I don't believe he would have the kind of control that he was used to having. And "reality TV"? I think HE WOULD HATE IT!!!

CHAPTER TWELVE

"I'll Ride the Wind" and
"The Wisdom of Solomon"

EXT. COUNTRYSIDE — DAY

John Jr. and Mary are walking hand in hand, talking about their future together. They cross a
small stream and John stops, turns.

          JOHN JR.
You know, we've been carrying on as if
it's all settled. I never even asked
you.

          MARY
Yes, you did.

          JOHN JR.
That was yesterday, when I was a boy.
     (he swallows)
I think I better ask you again.

          MARY
Go ahead.

          JOHN JR.
Mary Ingalls, I love you very much.
More than anything in the world. I
want you to be my wife.

          MARY
Thank you, John.

John and Mary kiss.

CONTINUED:

                    BILL CLAXTON (V.O.)
     Cut it! Once again.

WIDER ANGLE

We see the CAMERA CREW around Missy and Radames.
Bill Claxton, the director, walks over to them —
more specifically, over to *Missy*.

                    BILL CLAXTON
     Miss. Let's take a walk.

Missy knows this is a bad sign. She and Bill take
a walk away from the crew.

                    MISSY
     I'm sorry, Bill. I . . .

                    BILL CLAXTON
        (interrupting)
     Miss, you *are* an actress, right?

Missy nods, mortified.

                    BILL CLAXTON
     Then you need to put your personal
     feelings aside and just do your job,
     dear. I realize it's been awhile since I
     was thirteen and these kinds of scenes
     can be difficult. But *you* are better than
     this, Miss. And you *know* better.

Missy swallows hard, ashamed of herself.

                    BILL CLAXTON
     Now, I want you to do this scene
     again. We'll pick it up from "Thank
     you, John," and when you get to that
     kiss, *pretend* that you're attracted to
     the guy, okay?

CONTINUED:

Missy is relieved that the tirade has ended.

                    MISSY
        Yes, Bill. I'll do it better. I'm
        sorry.

They walk back to the crew, to "go again."

As I watch "I'll Ride The Wind," and this scene in particular, I am reminded of how difficult it is to be a teenager, let alone a girl growing up in front of millions of viewers.

This is a very good episode, written by Harold Swanton and beautifully acted by Radames Pera. My own acting, however, could have used some improvement. I don't remember who my teenage crush was at that particular time, but I was "in love" at one time or another with Bobby Sherman, David Cassidy, and Donny Osmond. Somehow Radames Pera just didn't rank on my "hunk" list.

When I watch this scene now, I attribute the brevity of the kiss more to the historical times, fortunately, than to my acting. In those days passion was reserved for after marriage. But Billy Claxton was right, and I learned a big lesson. I *did* let my personal feelings get in the way, and that kiss could have been a bit longer.

In the opening scene, we see a hawk soaring above. John Jr. wonders aloud to his adopted father, Isaiah Edwards, what the hawk must be thinking, feeling.

Edwards says, "Bet that's the difference between us. You're riding the wind, and me, I'm just riding a hay wagon."

I come running up to meet John with a letter that he's been waiting for. He had sent his collection of poetry to *The Pathfinder* publication, and they liked it.

John says, "They're going to buy my poems!"

At supper that evening, John tells his family all about it.

"I'm going to make a living at it, Pa." Edwards gives him a quizzical look, and John continues, "This'll *be* my work. Writin' poems and stories."

Edwards is incredulous. "Whaddya mean, you're gonna get up in the morning, drink your coffee, go off to work . . . with a pencil?"

John happily replies, "Yep, and write down the words and send 'em off to the publisher."

Edwards can't quite fathom this. "You can't make a livin' puttin' words down on paper."

Then John Jr. drops the "engagement" bomb. "Well, I'm gonna have to. Gonna have another mouth to feed pretty soon." At their shocked looks, John says, "I just asked Mary Ingalls to marry me, and she said she would."

Just as long as I never have to kiss him!

Over at the Little House, I let it slip—accidently, on purpose—that, "We're going to save our money and put it in the bank."

Pa says, "Who's we?"

I respond, "John and I."

Incredulous, Pa asks, "For what?"

I answer, "A house. A place of our own."

Shock.

I notice, watching this scene, that Mike's gray hair is showing through the brown. He was gray like a skunk—white, right down the middle. He used Clairol Loving Care shampoo-in hair color in medium ash brown. Larry Germain, our hairdresser, would hand him a box as a subtle hint whenever he needed freshening up.

Anyway, as the episode progresses, there is a scene shot completely in the wide-angle master, of Charles and Isaiah riding in the wagon across the countryside. Because no close shots were necessary, this entire scene was shot using their doubles: Hal Burton for Mike, and, I believe, Jack Lilley for Isaiah. The dialogue between the two men takes place in voice-over. They are talking about becoming in-laws. Since Charles won't let Mary marry until she is fifteen, they still have a year and a half to get used to the idea.

Edwards is trying to understand John Jr.'s world of writing. He tells Charles that he's not an authority on poetry but, "Seems like most of 'ems pretty well-off when they started. I mean, Byron was a Lord. Whaddya figure a Lord makes?"

Charles answers, "More than a farmer."

The man from *The Pathfinder* arrives to discuss John Junior's future. He tells John that he has the talent and the imagination but needs the discipline to shape it. Holding the book of poetry and short stories, he says, "It's a fine beginning, fine. But not yet ready for publishing."

Before anyone has much chance to react to this news, he offers John Jr. four years at the university: board, room, and tuition. That's a wow. John is thrilled. Grace is even more thrilled. Isaiah . . . not so much.

Edwards is hurt because he and his son are so different. When John offers to help with the chores, he says, "If you wanna be a poet, ya got no business pitchin' hay."

John says, "You don't want me to go."

Edwards responds, "Ya got better things to do than chores. Puttin' words down on paper. Now you can do that, you got no business farmin' or choppin' wood or pitchin' hay."

John says that he's only going away for awhile. "I'm not leaving you."

Edwards, out of the hurt he feels, replies, "We're different, boy. You and me, we're different. It's like we live on two different hills with a big ditch between us. You're doin' things I ain't got the faintest notion what they are." He concludes with, "I want you to be what you want to be. I ain't gonna pull you up on my hill if you want to stay on yours."

John Jr. comes out to my home to tell me his news. Charles misunderstands and thinks that John is there to officially "ask for my hand." When John finds out that I am not home, he runs off. Charles is baffled.

When he does find me, I am less than thrilled at the prospect of my (unofficial) fiancé being away in Chicago for four years. My heart is breaking.

John tells me, "We'll see each other twice a year."

I know that he will change, and I say, "It'll be like living on the moon compared to Walnut Grove." But truly, I want what's best for him.

He asks, "Are you sure you want me to go?"

I tell him, "When it's done, we'll both be glad you did it."

Now, John is unsure. He doesn't want things to change. To Grace, he says, "If I go away, I'll lose her."

She responds, "Maybe."

John says, "Things won't be the same again."

Grace says, "Things are *never* the same."

The next morning, John announces that he has made his decision. He's going to stay and farm with Isaiah. He's not going to take the scholarship. Grace pleads with him to go and seize this opportunity. Edwards is over the moon and tells John to go and get Mary because he has something he wants to show us.

Grace tries to persuade Isaiah to talk some sense into John, but Isaiah just says, "He made a man's decision."

Grace retorts, "A man's decision! A *boy* made it!"

John comes out to the house—misses me again. Charles, of course, thinks that *finally*, the time has come. John is here to talk to him. John runs off to catch up with me and Laura on our way to school. Charles is wrong, again.

John and I meet up with Edwards. He shows us the land he has been saving for John: eighty acres of our very own.

He tells us, "Ain't a better piece of bottom land in this whole state."

He intends to help John build our home there.

Finally, the big night has come! John Jr. is coming to talk to Pa. I am so nervous, I can't eat my dinner. John arrives, and he and Pa go outside for privacy.

John nervously says, "I love your daughter, sir."

To which Pa replies, "So do I."

Oh, come *on*, can he make it any harder on the poor guy?

Poor John finally gets through it, and Pa says, "Why don't you sit down before you fall down."

As John sits, relieved, Pa asks about the big decision John has recently made. Is he sure about giving up all of this? About his education?

John emphatically replies, "Yes, sir. I'm sure. I've made my decision."

Pa lets him know that when I am fifteen, he can have me.

Suddenly, I'm feeling like a piece of property.

John doesn't want anything more to do with writing. "I've got no time for books. I'm building a house."

Grace says, "He's empty. Something's gone out of him."

I approach Mr. Edwards at the site of the homestead. I explain that this has been a wonderful dream, but that, "What we're doing here is wrong."

Edwards responds, "You got yourself a good farmer down there. He's doin' it all for you."

I am crying when I say, "He *isn't* a farmer. He was born to books and words and the music he can make with them. And we're taking them away from him." When Edwards protests, I say, "He'll stay if we ask him to. With the life gone out of him. And the music."

We both want him to stay, but not that way.

We shot the Tag, or last scene, at the Jamestown Train Station that I mentioned earlier. Our two families are there to see John off.

Edwards and John take a moment. John thanks him, but Edwards quickly replies, "Ain't no reason to thank me. Debt's on my side. We'll be thinkin' about ya . . . all the time."

John and I have a tearful goodbye. I run along the platform as the train pulls out of the station. Boo, hoo. Edwards comes to me; we each feel as bad as the other.

As we worked our way through Season Three, our sweet and kind Karen Grassle was becoming a little less so. I'm not sure if this change in her personality was completely related to her dealings with Mike, but chances are that had a lot to do with it.

The first time I ever heard the infamous actor's quote: "What is my motivation for this scene?" followed by, "Your paycheck at the end of the week," from the director was in relation to Karen Grassle. Things had gotten to the point where the crew was talking about her behind her back.

Truth be told, she *was* really good in our show. She was a classically trained actress, which made her stand out in a town like L.A. She would have felt more at home in New York, I would think. That's not to say there aren't many great actors in L.A.; it's just that a lot of them have not had the kind of training that she had.

Mike Landon had taken some acting lessons early on, but by that time in his career, he relied on what he *knew* worked for him. He didn't take chances with his acting. I think that for the most part, this worked, but I've often wondered what kind of actor he could have been if he were guided by some great director in a project in which he wasn't holding the reins, so to speak.

I never thought Karen wanted fame as much as she wanted to be a great actress. The television industry is a tough place to be if one is unwilling to compromise his/her loftier aspirations. I remember hearing things from the crew like someone saying, "Good morning, Karen," and getting, "What's so good about it?" in return.

In her defense, I can imagine that it must have been difficult working on a show where the children are featured in most every episode. But she did sign on knowing this, and if Ed Friendly had stayed, she would have been pushed even further into the background. At least she could console herself with the fact that she had a steady gig and steady income. I can tell you she made a *lot* more money per episode than any of us kids did.

In those days, kids were not paid *nearly* what they would come to earn in subsequent years. It wasn't until shows featuring children in leading roles such as *Diff'rent Strokes*, starring Gary Coleman and my friend and *Little House* alum Todd Bridges, that kids really started raking in the bucks. These shows made so much money for the networks that they almost couldn't help but pay these kids accordingly. Frankly, it was about time. Child actors work hard.

Unfortunately for Karen, the more "divalike" her behavior became, the less likely it was that she would get a lot of meaty scenes to play. That's the way it worked: If you fell out of favor with Mike and company, they wanted you around as little as possible. But perhaps that was what she had in mind?

And so it went: a lot more of "More coffee, dear?" and "Close the door!" until one day, she stormed off the set and marched into her dressing room and stayed there. Wow. That was intense. I think it was Bill Claxton who got her to come out and go back to work, but believe me, this kind of behavior just didn't *happen* on Michael Landon Productions. And I never saw or heard of it happening again.

After I went blind on *Little House*, I worked less there and more on outside projects for other networks. I would come "home" to *Little House* every couple of months or so to work on a few episodes. On one of my first trips back, I noticed something strange. Mike and Karen were *smiling*. At each *other*. Weird. Was this real, or was it Memorex? I know, I'm dating myself again. Anyway, I never knew if it was in fact real or if they were simply acting. But it certainly made our set a lot less tense and a happier place to come back to.

Scott Swanton wrote the smart, sweet, and inspirational episode "The Wisdom of Solomon." Bill Claxton directed, and a friend of mine, Todd Bridges (we had the same agent), gave a magnificent performance. It starts with a very wide shot of a boy running. Running and running. We come to see that he is black and is being chased by a white man driving a buggy. The boy runs across a huge field being worked by his mother and much older brother. The man catches up and says that the boy stole a book from the school steps. He gets the boy's name and threatens to run the family out of town if it ever happens again. The boy, whose name is Solomon, pleads that he didn't mean to steal it. He just borrowed it. He wants to learn to read.

His mother tells him that they came here for a fresh start. "They'd have beat you half to death for that, back home."

Solomon says, "I wanna go to school like all them other children."

His mother explains that it's a white man's school; he can't go there.

"Why? If we're free, why can't I?" asks Solomon.

"You're free to be what the white folks want you to be," his mother replies sternly.

The boy challenges her, "If I can only be what the white folks want me to be, then I's a slave as much as Papa was."

His mother responds, "You do like I say and mind your place, or you can go."

That's all this head-strong kid needed to hear. He's outta there.

His mother yells after him, "You don't come back here now, you don't ever come back."

His older brother starts after him, but his mother says, "He done made up his mind."

The scene shifts to Mankato, where Charles and Dr. Baker are doing business. Another physician, Dr. Tane, helps Dr. Baker load crates of medicine into the wagon. In return, Baker will give Tane some of the many medicine samples he receives for Dr. Tane's work on the Indian Reservation.

Dr. Baker says, "I just don't understand why the government doesn't send proper medical supplies to the reservation?"

That gets a big laugh from Dr. Tane, and he replies, "Why should they? It's just for Indians."

Charles hears a scuffle. Solomon has been caught stealing an apple. Charles intervenes, tells the kid to ask next time, *gives* him the apple, and off Solomon goes. Charles and Dr. Baker start the trip back to Walnut Grove, but unbeknownst to them, they've got an extra seventy pounds in back, in the form of a little boy hitchin' a ride.

At school, Laura is daydreaming. As she pays no attention to what Miss Beadle is teaching, she sees, or *thinks* she sees, Solomon peeking through the schoolhouse window. It happens again. Yes, she definitely did see what she thought she saw. When she tells me, I don't believe her.

That night, when Laura goes to collect the eggs, she is shocked to find Solomon hiding with the chickens.

"Are you a for-real Negro person?" she asks. She tries to wipe the color from his cheek, can't believe it's there for good. "I've never seen a real Negro person before! Boy, is Miss Beadle gonna be sorry she didn't believe me."

Laura brings Solomon into the house where Ma gives him some supper. His name is Solomon Henry, and he was born in Mississippi and then lived in Virginia. He lies and says he has no family. He produces a piece of paper—dated 1854—advertising his father for sale as a slave. Solomon thinks he can do the same. He doesn't care that Lincoln signed the Emancipation Proclamation into law in 1863 because he believes that if he could sell himself as a slave, he'd earn money to go to school.

He says, "I wouldn't be much. You could name the price. Just so I had enough for a book or two. You wouldn't be sorry. I could work from sun up to sundown."

Pa says, "We'll fix you up with a place to sleep up in the soddy. You can do some chores to earn your keep. Tomorrow, I'll take you into town—see about getting you started in school."

When Charles says goodnight to the boy, Solomon tells him, "If you're a little shorta cash to buy me right off, you can always pay for me on time."

Morning comes. It's Solomon's first day of school, and Mrs. Oleson gives Charles a hard time regarding the boy. Charles gets the best of her, saying, "Solomon is my son by a former marriage." Ha. I believe this was more Mike's sense of humor than Charles Ingalls's.

Inside, Miss Beadle asks the children to write an essay on "The things you dislike the most." Answers range from cleaning the chicken coop to homework to "my sister."

Miss Beadle, trying to include Solomon in the discussion, asks, "Can you think of something that *you* dislike?"

Solomon thoughtfully answers, "Bein' a nigger."

Stunned silence fills the schoolhouse.

Charles goes back to Mankato to inquire if anyone around there knows Solomon or any family he might have. Unseen by Charles, Solomon's older brother overhears him asking.

At home, Laura feels guilty about her good life and that she takes her schooling for granted. That night, Charles asks Solomon about what he said at school. He tells Solomon that he must "start a new life now."

Solomon says, "Laws don't change nothin." He poses a question to Charles: "Would you rather be black and live to be a hundred? Or white and live to be fifty?"

Charles is speechless.

Solomon is doing very well in school. Ma says, "That boy may stay with us forever." She means she *wants* him to stay forever. We are all attached to him.

One night, Solomon's brother comes to fetch him back. He confronts Solomon in the little soddy where he sleeps, telling him that he should be working on those fifteen acres they have.

Solomon asserts, "I wanna learn to read. I wanna *know* things."

His brother asks angrily, "What good's it gonna do ya, huh?"

Solomon asks, "Is that all we're good for, Jackson? Working the field, day after day?"

They continue arguing, and Jackson says that nothing's gonna change.

"White folks ain't gonna let it change."

Solomon has learned from the "white folks." He trusts some of them and says, "I can be anything I want to be!"

"You wanna be white, boy?" his brother sneers. "Can't be that."

Solomon tells Jackson that if he makes him go home with him now, he'll just run away again. Jackson gives Solomon a package from his mother and tells him that he'll let her know he's safe.

One mornin, Charles rides into town with Solomon and waves hello to Dr. Baker and Dr. Tane. Solomon, surprised, says, "That black man's a doctor? *I'll* be a doctor."

He goes to talk to Dr. Tane. "You doctorin' around here?" Solomon asks, sincerely.

"You don't think white folks be lettin' me doctor 'em, do ya?"

Solomon looks crestfallen and feels completely let down.

The doctor sighs, then continues, "I'm a reservation doctor, boy. I do what I can for Indians, cause ain't no white doctor's gonna do it."

Solomon realizes the path his life will take and doesn't want to settle. He walks away sadly.

That evening, Caroline tells Charles that Solomon didn't want to eat, but she doesn't know what the matter is. Charles goes out to the Soddy to talk to him. Solomon is upset; things are never gonna change.

Charles tells him, "When people spend their whole lives thinkin' a certain way, it just takes time for 'em to change."

Solomon says, "We go to the same school, learn the same. But it don't make no difference. When we done, nothin's changed. All I'm still good for—walk behind a plow."

Charles says, "*I* walk behind a plow."

Solomon quickly asserts, "That's your choice. I ain't *got* a choice. Don't make no difference of learnin' somethin' if you can't use it. My mama and brother tried to tell me that." When he sees Charles's reaction, Solomon admits, "I've got a family."

Charles asks him why he didn't tell us.

"'Cause I wanted to be with you. Pretend you were my family. But it ain't no good pretendin'. I best be goin' tomorrow." The tears are spilling out of his eyes. Oh, this is sad, and Todd is *so* good.

The next day, Laura talks with Solomon. "What's wrong with people, Solomon? Why can't they change?"

Solomon replies, "Maybe in a hundred years or so things'll be different. Maybe."

I'm so proud that our show tackled this very important topic and in such eloquent fashion. I'm *extremely* proud that my country has elected its first African-American President. It's about time, and what a perfect person for the job. His youth and vitality will serve him and our country well in these difficult times. I'm grateful to the Obama campaign for bringing young Americans back into the fold. They know now that their voices will be heard and *listened* to, and they will therefore be more active in their roles as citizens of this great country.

But I digress.

Solomon goes to say goodbye to Miss Beadle and the children at school. He tells them what a good school this is: "You're mighty lucky to be able to come here. I'm thankful for being *allowed* to come here."

Those huge tears are falling down his face again, and now he's got Miss Beadle and me crying, too. He gives Miss Beadle a plaque that he's made. It's inscribed, "Bless This School." They cut to me just as a big tear falls down my face. The only one who isn't crying in this scene is, strangely, Laura. She is sitting there looking like nothing's happened. Hmmm. If I had edited this, I wouldn't have left that in.

The stagecoach has arrived that will take Solomon home. He gives Charles a big hug. Oh, this is too much. As I watch this, even *I* am sniffling. Now I see what everyone meant when they said that they always cried watching our show. I was too close to it then (and it wouldn't have been cool), but now . . . .

As I said earlier, Todd Bridges and I had the same "Mary Grady" representation. He was always an adorable kid—if a bit wild, which made it all the more amazing that he could calm down so quickly and turn in performances like this one.

He was obviously doing well (at least professionally) up to the time *Diff'rent Strokes* was cancelled in 1986. I don't know what happened to Todd after that. He got deeply involved with drugs and probably didn't have a good handle on who he was, deep down. *That,* I believe, is a common problem among us child stars. So much of our formative years are spent being *told* what to be; what we are expected to be. Outward appearances are everything. Not a lot of attention is paid to the stuff that doesn't show. But that's okay—it keeps us on our toes, gives us something to do when we're older—in therapy. I think that it's easy for us to not *ever* know who we really are without the lights, the makeup, and the fame.

There are many good things to be said about growing up on film, but it is risky, which is why I could never recommend it to anyone I care about. It's hard enough to be a teenager these days. Who needs the added pressure and the fear of not knowing if, after you manage to make your way through puberty, anyone will still want to hire you? Will your talent still be viable?

I was one of the fortunate few who got through those awkward years relatively unscathed. But I will tell you that if I hadn't, if producers hadn't wanted to hire me any more, I would have been heartbroken.

If I could advise child actors, I would say: Make sure you have something you can fall back on. Make sure your life doesn't only revolve around show business. Develop different interests and, most of all, get to know the great person that is way down deep. Spend your hard-earned money wisely. Furthering your education is a good idea. Make the most of the opportunity you've been given; appreciate it, but don't perceive it as the Be All, End All.

As for Todd, I am so happy and relieved that he continues to be clean and sober and out of trouble. I wish him only good things to come.

CHAPTER THIRTEEN

Blindsided

On *Little House,* we worked a five-day week when we shot in Los Angeles and a six-day week when we were on location. We worked a half day on Christmas Eve and a full day on Boxing Day (what Montrealers call the day after Christmas). We also worked on New Year's Eve and January 2nd.

I'm not sure if those hours were thought of as excessive at that time, but they sure would be now. Series television production actually comes to a halt during the holidays, giving everyone involved a nice little vacation. Families can enjoy their children's school breaks right along with them.

I never really minded our work schedule because I loved the work. Where I had trouble was with all of the publicity that I had to do. As I've mentioned, I was inherently shy, thus making this part of my job that much more difficult. If I was too quiet, that would be construed as snobbish. If my cheeks got sore from all of that smiling, people would think I was mad about something.

I liked and appreciated my fans, I truly did. But I *was* a kid, after all, and this just wasn't one of my favorite things to do. Having so much attention paid to my appearance and demeanor could be unnerving at times.

As I got older, the idea of traveling approximately one weekend out of most months, doing these personal appearances, became less and less appealing to me. I needed more time for myself—just to be a kid. I began to travel a bit less and spend more time at home doing telephone interviews. Much better.

I had many great times with my twin friends Pam and Tam. Linda and Mary Trescony (NBC executive Al Trescony's daughters) had become very close to me, as well. On many Saturdays when I was in town, the twins and I would get together and take a tennis lesson with David Dreben, our cute instructor. I'm convinced if we had paid as much attention to our form as we did to David's, we would actually be *good* players by now.

Afterwards we would go to our local shopping mall to look around. That was when we realized what kind of impact *Little House* was having. Kids would follow us around, getting very excited (to see me?) and finding whatever they could to have me autograph. Pam and Tam tell me that this was so cool; it's interesting for me to hear it from their perspective.

The rest of Saturday would be devoted to my "Fan Club." The twins ran the club, and there was always business to attend to. We'd read letters, adding a small personal note, if necessary, at the bottom of a continually updated form letter. I would personalize each autographed photo, etc., etc.

This was a strange task. It was fun and flattering to read these letters but also kind of embarrassing in front of my friends. Eventually it got easier—we had heard it all by that time! My fan mail was quite adorable: notebook paper folded three thousand times and stuffed into tiny envelopes. I received marriage proposals—some even included the ring!

One Saturday, I believe I was thirteenish, we took our usual tennis lesson with David Dreben and went to the mall. I had gotten better at the art of not attracting so much attention. I found that if I faced forward and went directly where I wanted to go and didn't dawdle, I could get around with less fuss.

When we got back to Pam and Tam's home, we did not work on the fan club; we instead got ready to go to a theater party that they had nicely invited me to. So we all spent the afternoon primping and fussing. This was back when Farrah Fawcett was huge, and I wanted nothing more than to have hair like hers. So, I trimmed my very own "wings" around my face and then had a professional fix it for me. I got away with this on *Little House* because my hair would still go into the combs on each side of my head; no one could tell.

I proudly flipped my new "wings" and put on seventies makeup for a change. Finally, we were all ready, and we all looked great. People used to say we looked like sisters—blonde and blue-eyed. But the twins were tall—over five-foot-eight—and I had to wear platform shoes to measure up.

It was early evening, I believe it was June, and it was still light out. The three of us climbed into their parent's big older-model Chevrolet. Pam was always the driver, I guess because she had the perfect eyesight of the two of them.

EXT. NEIGHBORHOOD STREETS — TRAVELING SHOT
— TWILIGHT

We see a big silver car turn onto a wide four-lane
street in a West Valley suburb of Los Angeles.

INT. CHEVROLET — TRAVELING — TWILIGHT

Pam is driving, Melissa beside her. Tam is in the
backseat.

           TAM
   Can we turn on the radio?

           MELISSA
   Oooh. Yeah. Okay, Pam?

           PAM
   Sure.

CONTINUED:

Melissa takes control of the radio. Punches the FM button and turns the dial to 102.7.

> MELISSA
> There, KISS FM. Good.

> RADIO ANNOUNCER
> Hey, there. This is Rick Dees, and just in case you didn't know or couldn't guess what the number one song of the week is, I'll play it for you. Here she comes, her fifth week in a row . . .

> PAM, TAM, & MELISSA
> (interrupting Rick)
> Oooh! Oh, good!

> RICK DEES
> (continuing)
> Miss Debby Boone and "You Light Up My Life."

Melissa turns up the VOLUME on the radio.

> DEBBY BOONE
> (singing)
> So many nights I sit by my window
> Waiting for someone to sing me his song . . .
> So many dreams I kept deep inside me
> Alone in the dark but now
> you've come along . . .

> DEBBY, PAM, TAM, AND MELISSA
> (the girls join in and sing full-
> out at the top of their voices)
> You light up my life
> You give me hope
> To carry on

CONTINUED:

                    DEBBY BOONE (CON'T)
        You light up my days
                (the girls get more dramatic here)
        And fill my nights with song

EXT. STREET — TWILIGHT

The Chevy drives down the street. A POLICE CAR
turns onto the boulevard behind the Chevy.

INT. CHEVROLET — TRAVELING — TWILIGHT

The three happy girls are still singing. Melissa
turns up the volume a bit more.

                    DEBBY, PAM, TAM, AND MELISSA
        . . . Finally, a chance to say
                (with great drama)
        Hey, I love you
        Never again to be all alone

EXT. STREET — TWILIGHT

We can HEAR the SINGING from outside the Chevy as
it rolls along. The Chevy goes right through a
STOP SIGN and continues along, unscathed. We can
see the Police Car's rolling RED LIGHTS GO ON.

INT. POLICE CAR — TRAVELING — TWILIGHT

The POLICEMAN is surprised that this car hasn't
stopped, but is not trying to get away. He picks
up his RADIO.

CONTINUED:

                    POLICEMAN
              (into radio)
      Yeah. This is Three-Charlie-Fourteen.
      Need you to run a plate on a sixty-
      eight, maybe seventy, Chevrolet
      Caprice, Henry, Charlie, Thomas . . .

INT. CHEVROLET — TRAVELING — TWILIGHT

                    DEBBY, PAM, TAM, AND MELISSA
              (still singing loudly)
      'Cause you, yoo-ooo light up my life
      You give me hope
      To carry on-nnnn
      You light up my days
      And fill my nights with song

EXT. STREET — TWILIGHT

The silver Chevrolet is still being followed by
the police car with LIGHTS and now SIREN WAILING,
as well.

INT. POLICE CAR — TRAVELING — TWILIGHT

As our Policeman gets the all-clear from the
station:

                    POLICEMAN
      That's a ten-four. No warrants. I'll
      keep you updated.

INT. CHEVROLET — TRAVELING — TWILIGHT

And the girls are (what else?) still singing. Going
for their Big Finish, giving it all they've got:

CONTINUED:

>   DEBBY, PAM, TAM, AND MELISSA
>   It can't be wrong
>   When it fee-eels so right
>   'Cause you
>   You light up my-yyyy life.

And just as Melissa turns the radio volume down, the girls notice, not to mention HEAR, the SIREN and LIGHTS coming from behind.

>   PAM, TAM, AND MELISSA
>   (in unison)
>   Oh no!

Melissa quickly turns the radio off as Pam finally pulls the car over to the side of the road.

EXT. STREET — TWILIGHT

The police car follows suit. The Policeman gets out of his car, hand on his holstered firearm, and proceeds determinedly to the Chevrolet.

INT. CHEVROLET — TWILIGHT

Pam nervously rolls down her window, with dread. ANGLE INCLUDES the Policeman leaning in at the window.

>   POLICEMAN
>   License and registration, Miss.

Pam fumbles for her driver's license and hands it to him.

>   POLICEMAN
>   And your registration, please.

CONTINUED:

                    PAM
          Oh! Oh! Yes! Sorry!

Pam opens the glove compartment to search for the
registration. The policeman looks at Melissa and Tam.

                    POLICEMAN
          Do you know how long I've been behind
          you?

It has dawned on the girls what has happened.

                    TAM
          We had the radio on. We were singing.
          We're sorry.

Pam finds the registration and hands it to him.

                    POLICEMAN
          You ran a stop sign back there. I've
          been following you for over a mile.

                    PAM
          Oh! No, I didn't see it! Oh!

                    POLICEMAN
          Well, you'll be sure to see it the
          next time, won't you? And you'll know
          better than to listen to your music so
          loudly. Don't go away, I'll be right
          back.

He walks back to his car to write the ticket. You
don't fool around with the L.A. police.

                    MELISSA
          Thank God he didn't recognize me. My
          Farrah wings must've thrown him off.
          I'm so embarrassed, I would have died.

CONTINUED:

EXT. STREET — TWILIGHT

The Policeman starts walking back as he finishes
writing the ticket.

INT. CHEVROLET — TWILIGHT

As the Policeman reaches the open window:

>   PAM
>   I didn't see a stop sign. Did you see
>   a stop sign? I wouldn't have missed
>   that. It must have been hidden by a
>   tree.

The policeman clears his throat. Pam turns, gulps,
hoping she hasn't just made her situation even
worse.

>   POLICEMAN
>   Here you are, miss.

He hands her the ticket.

>   PAM
>   Thank you.

>   POLICEMAN
>   You have a good evening, now.

We had a great time at the party. I loved being included in their
group of friends. And we were very careful driving home!

By the way, Pam still insists to this day that that stop sign was
covered by tree branches.

About halfway through the third season, I started to hear rumblings about my character going blind. I always knew that this could happen. It was written in the original *Little House* books, but after the split between Mike and Ed Friendly, I thought that maybe I'd somehow dodged this bullet. After all, that was what their rift was about: staying true to the books, or moving away creatively, to increase the drama and the longevity of our show.

I was sure that if they made Mary blind, I would have to be written out of the series. What else could they do? As I remembered the books, there wasn't much about Mary after she lost her sight. I started to worry. And I worried and worried. I loved my job. I loved going to work each day. It was my niche. I really felt as though I had learned so much so far, and I couldn't bear the thought of it all coming to an end.

I somehow made it through the rest of the season, and I was grateful for the two jobs I had lined up for this hiatus: *Very Good Friends* and *James at 15*. If I didn't have a regular series job, I might have to get used to doing freelance acting again.

We wrapped the third season in February 1977, I finally got up the nerve to confront Mike directly and find out for myself, once and for all, the fate of my character. It's interesting that I use the word "confront" as I have *never* been one for confrontation. I avoid it at all costs.

When we finished shooting that day, the wrap party was set up on our soundstage at Paramount Studios. It was a huge, sprawling space—two gigantic soundstages put together—where we could shoot scenes in the house, the barn, Oleson's Mercantile, Mary and Laura's little loft, and the church, which doubled as the school. It was like an enormous warehouse with overhead lights and padded walls to muffle any outside sounds.

It was a bare-bones wrap party. They probably spent more on the liquor than they did on the food—a couple of tables with super-long deli sandwiches. I spotted Mike across the stage and headed in his direction. My heart was racing, and my stomach was tied up in a huge knot.

"Um . . . Uh . . . Hey, Mike?"

He turned, saw me, and smiled. "Hey, darlin'. How ya doing?"

"Uh, well, good . . . I guess." I was now having trouble looking him in the eye.

"Something on your mind, Missy?"

And then, out it came. "Is it true? Are you really going to make me go blind next season?"

I waited for what seemed forever for my answer.

"Yes, Missy, you will be going blind next season."

My heart sank. I felt sick. The tears sprang up and out before I even had time to digest this news. I couldn't hold them back. I madly tried to think of something, anything else, so I would stop crying and not humiliate myself any further.

Just about the time I almost really lost it, Mike said, "Don't worry, Missy. It's going to be great. You'll see." He gave me a big hug.

"R-r-really?" I sobbed. "You're not going to write me out?"

"Of course not," he said. "You were so good in 'Soldier's Return.' And the work you did with Johnny Cash. . . . You really carried that show, and he raved about what a pro you are."

It was as if he wasn't sure whether I was afraid of being written out or afraid that I couldn't handle portraying a blind girl. He wanted to reassure me about both. He then told me how much he thought of my acting (*my* acting?) and how he saw that I was using every opportunity to learn more. He knew that I was serious about being an actress when I was older.

"You have a great future ahead," he told me.

I was sure he wasn't just saying that to make me feel better; he wasn't that kind of guy. He didn't sugarcoat anything, and he always said what he meant. He went on to explain what would happen to

Mary and the show and how he *knew* this would be a great opportunity for me. I trusted Mike and chose to accept the wonderful feeling of relief that had come over me.

Very Good Friends was an ABC Afterschool Special produced by Martin Tahse. Martin is one of the true gentlemen TV producers. The other was Aaron Spelling. Both of these men sent me "Thank You" notes after we'd wrapped each respective production. I doubt that kind of thing happens much any more. *Very Good Friends* was written by Arthur Heinemann (a frequent *Little House* writer) and directed by Richard Bennett. It went on to win the Golden Hugo at the Chicago Film Festival and the Gabriel Award recognizing broadcasting excellence.

James at 15, written by Dan Wakefield and directed by Joseph Hardy, was a two-hour movie pilot for NBC. Because I was hired as guest-star, I wouldn't have to participate if it sold and went to series, which it did. It was the highest-rated movie on television that week. I was happy for Lance, and we had a great time shooting this. We filmed fun (and funny) dream sequences, and from what I gather, our sleeping bag scene is quite infamous. Another interesting note: *Little House's* Jesse James (handsome actor Dennis Rucker) was Tiger in this movie.

I only had a total of ten days left of my hiatus to spend on vacation—in the Bahamas—no, just kidding, back at my regular high school in Flintridge, California. Then it was business as usual—back at the Little House.

SEASON FOUR
May 1977–January 1978

CHAPTER FOURTEEN

"Times of Change," "The Handyman," and "The Aftermath"

"Times of Change," written by Carole and Michael Raschella and directed by Bill Claxton, was a bit of a departure for us. We shot a lot of this episode at Twentieth Century Fox, using the great period streets on their back lot. Fox was definitely *my* favorite studio to shoot at because they had the nicest commissary—with the best food. I knew this because *The Love Boat* was shot there, and I had gotten a taste (literally) of this good life when I worked for Aaron Spelling. Sadly, our Paramount commissary was pretty dingy in those days, and the food . . . well, it filled the gap at lunchtime and that's about it. At Fox, I would often skip over the delicious entrees and go straight for the frozen yogurt. Frozen yogurt was new and hard to come by in those days, but Fox had it. Yum. It was also fun to eat lunch in a nice atmosphere—just like a nice restaurant, carpeted, with potted plants and trees. I ate with not only the usual actor types but with many executives as well. This really *was* a restaurant if the "suits" ate there.

The episode begins with Mary reading a letter from John, who's still away at the University in Chicago. He mentions the school's annual cotillion. He would love to be able to escort me but knows that is impossible. Charles has big news to share: he will represent Walnut Grove at the Grange Convention, and he is quite excited about it. He wants Caroline to go with him.

When he sees me "down in the dumps," he asks what the matter is. I tell him that I miss John. It's been so long since I last saw him. He didn't even get back for Christmas. It's already spring. Pa tells me that the convention will take place in Chicago, and I immediately jump on that. He and Ma will be able to find out how John is doing, how he looks. They can give him that shirt I made for him for Christmas. I run up to the loft to get it.

"It will be almost as if I was really there," I say.

Caroline talks to Charles. Although she'd love to make this trip with him, she'd rather that it be me. She says, "I can see Chicago on a picture-postcard."

She wants me to be able to spend time with John. There's a good mom for ya.

Caroline goes to her trunk, pulls out a beautiful dress, and proceeds to tell me the story behind it. It seems she wore it for Pa before they were married. He took one look at it and said, "Caroline, you are the prettiest thing this side of heaven."

She smiles at the memory. Then she says, "I fell in love with him at that moment, and I've loved him ever since."

Now, I smile, and she says, "Maybe you should try it on, see if it needs any adjusting."

I ask, "Why are you giving it to me?"

With a *really* big smile, she responds, "You're going to need something nice for the cotillion."

We use a stock shot (film footage that is kept to be used over and over whenever necessary) of the exterior of that Jamestown Steam Train and cut to the interior, shot at Paramount, where Pa and I are boarding. We get to our seats in coach, but before we know it, we are being whisked off to First Class! It's a lovely compartment, compliments of the Grange.

"We're gonna ride in style," Pa says.

The train chugs along. Our lunch arrives on a silver tray.

This is strange: I don't remember shooting this scene at all.

When we arrive at our hotel, I see a woman with a small dog and say to Pa, "That dog has a coat on."

Pa grabs our luggage and carries it into the hotel. The bellman just shakes his head: "Another farmer."

When we go to check in, we are told, "Your accommodations are paid in full." We are shocked. That Grange again.

We are shown to a magnificent suite of rooms with beautiful furnishings. "I never had my own room before," I say in wonderment. Are we lucky, or what?

We go to meet John at the *Chicago Register*, where he works. I can't get over the fact that he works for such a big newspaper. We meet John's boss and accept his invitation to dine with him that evening. I finally am able to give John his Christmas gift: the shirt I made for him.

Charles attends his first meeting of the Grange. After the chairman calls the meeting to order, he asks those in attendance: "How do you feel about the Grange?" The response? Whoops, hollers, whistles. No wonder!

At dinner, John is evasive when questioned about visiting Walnut Grove. He doesn't feel it necessary to show me the university, either. But the evening is wonderful, and the food is delicious, so Pa and I are really enjoying ourselves.

The next morning, as John and I are walking, he buys me my first piece of chewing gum, and I like it. We run into Wesley, a friend of John's from school. He calls me "The Country Girl." I'm not sure how much I like that. Wesley reminds John about an appointment he has with Miss Lawrence. John thanks him and tells me that she's one of his professors and that he'll see me later. Wesley will escort me back to the hotel.

John is late for his "appointment" with a very pretty city girl. She is holding a large box that contains the dress that she's bought to wear to the cotillion. She asks John to pick her up at seven.

I'm being two-timed!

City Girl notices John's new shirt and remarks, "Where in heaven's name did you get that silly shirt? You look like a farmer!"

At the hotel that night, Charles gets a very unexpected visit from a "lady of the evening" who has been sent by Stanley Hollister, an executive with the railroad. Charles is doubly mortified that this is happening in front of his daughter. He sends her packing.

At the Grange meeting, a Mr. O'Connell, says, "Got Hollister's 'message', huh?" He tells Charles that he might just get that grain elevator needed in Springfield if Charles can manage a "no" vote on state regulation. Charles is flabbergasted. Why in the world would he do a thing like that? He looks around at the drunken men with their "women" and realizes that nothing's going to be accomplished on this night. The Grange and the railroads are corrupt; making deals under the table and taking bribes. He's seen enough; he leaves.

The next evening is cotillion night. When I enter in my pretty dress, Pa tells me, "I've always been proud to be your father, but never as proud as I am tonight." He starts to pin on the corsage that John sent and says, "You look beautiful."

Pa and I arrive at the cotillion, and John finds us. He asks Charles to pick me up because he is covering this dance for his paper and must leave early.

I'll bet.

John dances with me. I thank him for the flowers and say, "I love you, John."

Nothing.

John's friend Wesley cuts in. John goes off to dance with "City Girl." She is angry at John because he's acting odd and keeps leaving her. She marches off. John comes back to me.

Meanwhile, Charles attends another meeting of the Grange. He has become increasingly frustrated with the way things are done here in the big city. He has finally come to the end of his rope. He jumps up, interrupting the meeting, "Why waste your time being honest when you can make so much more money by being dishonest?"

The chairman tells him he's out of order.

Charles angrily shouts: "I didn't come to Chicago on a load of hay!"

They are yelling and telling him to sit down. He continues, "This dumb farmer's gonna vote *yes* on state regulation, and I don't care *what* it costs."

Back at the dance, John goes to get us some punch. "City Girl" appears and apologizes to John for what occurred earlier. He sends *her* out to the terrace while getting *me* the punch. Just when you thought things couldn't get any more complicated, Charles walks in, sees John across the room and follows him out to the . . . terrace.

How ya gonna get outta this one, Johnny boy?

Charles has seen all he needs to see by the time John notices him standing there. He makes "City Girl" leave. She's mad, again. "I've had a bad evening, young man, and right now, I'm about as angry as I've ever been in my life," he says.

"I know, sir," John says, meekly.

Charles asks angrily, "What kinda game are you playin'?"

John begins to reply, he didn't know we were coming, etc. . . . But Charles interrupts with: "Are you in love with my daughter?"

After what seems like an eternity, John replies, "No, sir."

John goes on to say that when you're far apart, it's easy to avoid knowing the truth. He was going to write me a letter.

A *letter*? A "Dear Mary" letter? What a cad! What a coward!

Charles can't believe what he's hearing and says, "John, Mary has a right to hear it from you. She has a right to tell you how she feels. I think you owe her that much."

You bet he does.

In our lovely suite at the hotel, I have collapsed in a puddle of tears on that big, beautiful bed. Pa enters and sits down on the bed next to me. I tell him that I *believed* his letters. To which Pa responds, "Maybe he just wrote you the things that he thought you wanted to hear."

I sob, "But I feel the same, Pa. I love John."

Pa says, "But he's not the same, darlin'. He's changed. He's different. He's a city boy, now. He has different needs."

And then, I say the words that are every parent's worst nightmare: "I could learn to be what he needs. I could change, too."

Nooooo!

Pa tries to console me, saying, "There's only one thing in this world you can do better than anyone else."

Sniffle. "What?"

"Just be yourself."

I can only sob. And sob. And sob.

My nose was running all over Mike's shoulder.

Pa says, "Why don't we go home? I just don't think you and I belong here."

Back on the train. Coach this time.

Pa remarks, "Don't think they'll be servin' us any fancy lunch."

I just want to get home. As luck would have it, a boy comes and sits across from us. He offers us sandwiches that his ma made. We make small talk. He's nice. We introduce ourselves. We talk some more. He doesn't live too far from us. We keep talking. And talking. And talking. Pa watches, smiles knowingly. He knew best.

Seeing Mike Lookinland again, in "Times of Change," reminds me of the *Brady Bunch* episode I shot in 1973. *The Brady Bunch* was my first real "part." I had only acted in television commercials before that. I was

This boy was played by Mike Lookinland, who was my first screen kiss in an episode of *The Brady Bunch*. It was terrific to work with him again. He was just as nice as he had been years before. I was surprised to see his hair blond and curly; he told me that they always made him dye his hair dark and straighten it for his role as Bobby on *The Brady Bunch,* so that all of the boys would look like their TV dad, Robert Reed. Who knew?

ecstatic to be cast as Bobby's first love, Millicent. When the director, Lloyd Schwartz, saw my long blonde hair, he quickly added a dream sequence to the episode that parodied a famous Clairol shampoo commercial from the '70s, having Mike and me run to each other in slow motion. As two young kids, we were kind of embarrassed to do this, but it really did turn out to be a fun episode. I remember watching it on TV and being shocked by my *voice*. I knew what I looked like on film, but I had never heard so much of my voice before. I thought: *That's* what I sound like? Very high-pitched and California. Ick. I vowed to work on lowering it right there and then.

I never had a copy of that *Brady Bunch,* and I really wanted to be able to show it to my children. I ran into Lloyd Schwartz at Theater West in Los Angeles and asked him if he had any thoughts about how I could obtain a copy. He told me that he'd talk to his dad, Sherwood (creator of *Brady Bunch* and *Gilligan's Island*), and maybe his dad would give me a copy. How great, I thought. One day, not long after that conversation, my phone rang, and Sherwood Schwartz was calling. He was very nice, and we chatted for quite a while before he said that he didn't have any idea when the season with my episode of the *Brady Bunch* would be released on video. I think his son, Lloyd, had presumed that Sherwood would just run me off a copy from his master tapes of the show. Oh, well. A few years later, Patrick Loubatiere, a French author and journalist, found a copy and kindly sent it to me. My kids both loved it, by the way, and I now think I was just as cute as a button back then. The voice doesn't seem so bad, either!

"The Handyman" guest-starred Gil Gerard, who would go on to become NBC's "Buck Rogers." It was written by Arthur Heinemann and directed by Bill Claxton.

Charles is building us a bigger kitchen, complete with a sink and water pump. No more carrying buckets of water from the creek. The work is progressing well, but we still are minus one wall, in the back, when Charles receives word that he must go on the road with work for Mr. Hanson. He won't be able to finish the project at home, but they can use the extra money. A giant storm blows in and the rain is pounding down as Charles and Caroline nail a large tarp over the gaping hole in the kitchen.

He laughs and says, "You were gonna wash the floors, anyway!"

He leaves the next morning and expects to be away for at least two weeks.

One day, Caroline hears someone whistling at the back of her home. She finds Chris Nelson, the handsome handyman, examining the new kitchen in progress. Nels Oleson has sent him, knowing we had lots of unfinished work to do. Chris is a carpenter and can fix just about anything. Money doesn't seem to be too important—he was working for meals at the Mercantile.

Caroline and Chris strike a deal: "Whatever you're willin' to pay is fine. I work at my own pace and eat and sleep where I find myself."

"You'll eat with us," Caroline says. And he can sleep in the soddy.

After a great supper, Chris says, "I hope your husband realizes what a lucky man he is."

Caroline smiles.

Chris even works at night, by lantern light. Caroline goes out to tell him he must stop or risk waking the children.

"You do very good work," Caroline compliments him.

Chris replies, "I do the best I can. Actually, I'm just tryin' to match the work your husband did."

Caroline says, "You just go from town to town, is that it?"

He says that he likes wanderin'. "Up 'til now, I haven't found a place I'd like to nail my boots to the floor in."

The next morning, I remark: "Ma said it must be lonely, wanderin'."

He responds, "Well, I got to know a lot of people, but not, as you might say, close."

After breakfast, Chris is prepared to start his day's work. Caroline explains that it is Sunday and lets Chris know in no uncertain terms that "You're not doing work around here on the Lord's day."

So, Chris accompanies us to church, and Mrs. Oleson sneers, "My, how cozy." I overhear this and stop. She continues, "Just like one of the family, isn't he?"

That night Chris knocks at our door. Caroline answers, in her robe. She politely doesn't let him in, but talks at the door. He feels badly about what Mrs. O. said earlier and wondered if it had bothered Caroline. She says not to worry. She's used to Mrs. Oleson.

"See you in the morning," she says.

Before he leaves, Chris compliments Caroline on her lovely long hair. Karen had short hair and always wore this long wig for nighttime scenes.

"It's beautiful that way," he says.

Has Mary overheard *this* exchange as well?

One day shortly after, it's lunchtime at school, and Nellie decides she hasn't been mean enough lately and says, "When the cat's away, the mice do play." Laura and I don't really know what she means. "I'll bet your mother knows," Nellie says. And then she adds, "Some folks call it 'monkey business.'"

Laura is still in the dark. But not me. As Nellie taunts, "Monkey business, monkey business . . ." I've had it. I haul off and slap her but good. Right across her face. I heard later that the audience loved that.

In the meantime, Chris has fallen off our roof. Ma, of course, insists on fixing him up. She must mend the sleeve of his shirt, so she loans him one of Charles's. He compliments her on her pretty long hair again. She says, "Well, it wouldn't be very practical working around here with it like that."

Chris comes back with, "Might not be very practical, but it'd sure be pretty to look at."

She smiles again.

When I arrive home from school and see Chris wearing Pa's shirt, ooh, am I mad.

I confront Ma: "I wanna know why *he's* wearin' the shirt I made for Pa?"

When she explains about his fall, I apologize, but I really want this guy gone.

Pa returns to pick up another shipment for Hanson but must leave again right away. On his way back, Mrs. Oleson has said all kinds of things to Charles about our handyman, trying to make him jealous. Chris seems to have made himself scarce. Hmm. Pa is impressed with the work Chris has done so far, but Caroline is slightly miffed that he doesn't seem to be jealous even a little bit. I tell Pa I don't want him to go.

Chris, on the other hand, *is* jealous of Charles and our family. He says to her, "This is not my house and not my family." Poor Caroline is getting it from both sides.

Chris later finds Caroline at the creek and apologizes. He slowly says, "This past couple of weeks . . . I started feeling like you really were my family . . . *all* of you."

"I just think it shows you're not the kind of man you thought you were. You don't like wandering as much as you say," she says.

Caroline slips on the creek bank, but luckily, is caught by Chris. Naturally, nosy me has walked up at that precise moment, just in time to see the "catching" part, which to me looks suspiciously like an embrace. Oh. Oh. And you thought I was mad before.

I sneak out of the house that night and pay our handyman a little visit. I tell him in no uncertain terms that I want him outta here ASAP. I accuse him of being in love with Ma, to which he sadly says, "I'll be gone by morning."

Well, that's that.

When morning comes and the rest of my family realizes Chris has gone, a subtle look of satisfaction comes across my face. Ma figures something's up and asks me to tell what I know. I proceed to raise my voice to her—*not* a good idea—and say that I saw the two of them by the creek. I rant on and on. I tell her that Chris loves her. He couldn't deny it.

She finally has a chance to talk: "And that's why he's gone?"

I answer, "Yes. Yes and I'm glad. I never want to see him again."

Ma then explains just how much she loves Pa—more than anything in the world. Of my insinuations, she says, "I am *shocked* and hurt that you would think such a thing."

I, of course, feel terrible—and so I should. I apologize and we hug. Enough apologies in this show?

Ma and I go to try and find Chris. When we do, I, well, you know. I apologize—again. He says he's not sure where he'll go now. "Maybe I'll try to find me a woman like your Ma."

Caroline smiles.

Pa returns. He can have the kitchen finished in two weeks. He goes on and on about the work, the sink, and just when Caroline is about to lose all hope, he says, "Hey, your hair looks pretty that way." She blushes, hugs him. Her hair is down, the way the handyman liked it.

I worked with John Bennett Perry, Matthew's father—the "Old Spice" man—on "The Aftermath." I really liked this episode, written by Don Balluck, directed by Bill Claxton, and I've enjoyed getting to revisit it for this book.

The show starts with me explaining our class project to Pa while we are riding along in the wagon. We are going to examine the Civil War from both sides to try and get a balanced look at things. Pa doesn't think that it's a good idea necessarily, as the war has only been over for eleven years. Folks are settling in around Walnut Grove from both sides.

The stage comes galloping in with the big news that the James Brothers tried to rob another bank and that two members of their gang were shot dead and Frank James was wounded, but the James brothers managed to escape capture. As our townspeople read the story in the newspaper that's just come in off the stage, passengers disembark, get their luggage, and walk away.

One man, a Mr. Hobbs, sits on a bench outside the Post Office. He almost passes out when his friend, who is unloading at the stage-coach, sees and rushes to his side. Pa and I have stopped to see what all the commotion is about and end up meeting these two men with Mr. Hanson, who will rent them a house in Walnut Grove. We ask if Mr. Hobbs needs a doctor. His friend, Mr. Dankworth, played by Dennis Rucker, says Hobbs just needs time and rest for his swamp fever. He doesn't want to see a doctor.

Pa and I help the two men settle in to their rental. They want to hire me, at ten cents a day, to run errands for them while Mr. Dank-worth looks after Mr. Hobbs and he recovers from his swamp fever.

After we leave, Mr. Hobbs/Frank James says, "Jesse, we were sure lucky I didn't pass out back there."

Mr. Dankworth (Jesse) tends to Frank's gunshot wound: "We've had our own way for a long time, Frank."

Frank winces but is relieved to know that the bullet went through. Thoughtfully, he asks, "Is it all over, Jesse?"

Jesse replies, "Well, things never be like they always were. Just you and me, now." And finally, "We started life as farmers. We can be farmers again."

"Think I'm ready for that," sighs Frank.

"You and me, both," Jesse agrees.

At school, arguments are breaking out—just like Pa feared they would. I get into it with a kid named Bobby, who says, "The whole South is nothin' but a bunch of rebels and murderers."

I talk to Mr. Hobbs and Mr. Dankworth about the war. The two fought for the South. I tell them that's great because the point of view at school seems to always be from the North.

Frank says, "In a war, people do terrible things to each other."

They tell me I should take a look at "Rule Eleven" passed in 1863.

Bounty hunters have arrived in Walnut Grove, offering a reward for the James Brothers. Charles takes a look at the "wanted" poster—it's *them*. But Charles knows that with these bounty hunters, the brothers don't stand a chance of getting a fair trial. Or any trial at all, for that matter.

At their rented house, Jesse is at the window as the bounty hunters ride out of town. He doesn't think anyone suspects anything. Frank says, "Even so, I say we should buy a couple of horses and head on outta here tonight."

Jesse says, "Frank, they've been here and gone. I'd say this is the safest place we could be right now."

Boy, was he wrong.

There is a town meeting, and it's decided that Charles will go to Mankato to notify the marshal there. But the bounty hunters have returned. They have a witness who says he *knows* they got off the stage in Walnut Grove last week. Where *are* they?

The Reverend Alden suggests they have (another) town meeting to stall for time. He says, "If we're to turn these men in for execution without a trial, it's going to be the decision of every member of this community—not just ours."

Back at the house, Jesse and Frank are understandably worried. Jesse says, "I don't know about you, Frank, but that bunch won't be takin' *me* alive."

Jonathan Garvey, played by the late Merlin Olsen, former defensive tackle for the Los Angeles Rams, comes to our schoolhouse and talks with Miss Beadle. She quickly dismisses everyone early. She tells me that I've done excellent work on this project. I couldn't have, without the help of Hobbs and Dankworth, I think to myself.

I tell Laura that I'm going to stop by their house and thank them on my way home. Pa only told me I couldn't *work* for them. He never said I couldn't talk to them.

Laura warns, "I don't think you should."

I go anyway.

Laura sees Pa and has to tell him where I went.

Good thing.

Jesse James is looking out the window as I approach and walk up to the door.

"Take a look," says Jesse.

Frank says, urgently, "No, Jesse, no."

Jesse just says, "Life's hard, Frank. We use what means we can to stay alive. That girl might be the only way we have."

Frank lowers the shades on the windows. "There's gotta be another way."

Jesse explains that they have no horses, not to mention Frank's bad leg. They have now taken a hostage—unfortunately it's me.

Frank says, resigned, "All right, Jesse. All right."

The camera pushes in on my petrified face: "Unless they let you go, you'll . . . you'll *kill* me?"

Jesse shuts me up; he puts me in a closet.

Charles sneaks out of the mill office window and lowers himself into the murky creek below. He manages to hide among the tall reeds while Garvey diverts the bounty hunters' attention.

At the house, Frank says, "A hostage is no good unless you're willing to kill that hostage. Are you willing to do that?"

Jesse replies simply, "We have to be."

Back to Charles—now he is swimming.

The town meeting is heated. Garvey tells everyone that I am being held hostage. "We can't say nothin', or they might kill her."

Reverend Alden says, "As minister of this congregation, I will condone *any* act, *any statement* designed to protect the life of Mary

Ingalls. Now, may God forgive me if I'm wrong, but under the circumstances, that's the least I can do. Now we will unite and be one in this . . ."

His voice trails off as he sees the shadow of Broder, the bounty hunter, slowly walking into the church. He reminds the townspeople of that reward. Lets them know that it's five thousand dollars. *Half* of that is a lot of money.

Charles has finally made it to the house where the James Brothers are holed up. Pointing a gun at him, they take him hostage, too.

In the church, one man, that Bobby kid's father, almost spills the beans to Broder, at least in part, to get that reward. Garvey knocks the man out with one punch. *I* wouldn't want to be getting in Merlin Olsen's face, would you?

Garvey makes Broder promise not to hurt me and, doing his best impression of a bad guy, says he better "get his half of that reward money," 'cause *he'll* show the posse where those Brothers have hid out. He proceeds to take the posse on a wild goose chase.

While Broder and team get into position to lure the brothers out, Garvey unties all of their horses and spooks them so they run off.

The bounty hunters fire on an empty house, and now they have no horses, either.

Garvey has gone to the James's house with two of the horses. As the James Brothers get ready to ride out, Jesse apologizes to me. Garvey says, "Listen, if I was you two, I'd be ridin' while I still had a skin on."

They ride off.

Pa says quietly, "Thank you, Jonathan."

The three of us, me, Pa, and Garvey, leading a stray horse, walk back into town.

Garvey explains to Broder, "All that shootin' up there spooked the horses somethin' terrible, and me and Charles, we had a horrible time tryin' to run 'em down." And, finally, he says, "Oh, uh, Broder, you got them outlaws, didn't ya?"

He waits for the posse to go, then smiles. So do we.

Cut to the interior of the church, and me in my "pizza" hat that I hated. It was round and flat and reminded me of a pizza. I look back over the rows of pews to Bobby and his father, as the camera pushes in on Bobby's face.

In voiceover I say, "The James Brothers made good their escape, and none of us ever saw them again. Except Bobby Ford, who would see Jesse another day; his last day, six years later."

On the screen we see the words:

JESSE JAMES WAS SHOT AND KILLED BY BOB FORD ON APRIL 3, 1882, IN ST. JOSEPH, MISSOURI.

CHAPTER FIFTEEN

"I'll Be Waving as You Drive Away"
Parts 1 & 2

About a month before shooting our last two episodes of the season, I received the scripts for the two-part episode: "I'll Be Waving As You Drive Away," beautifully written by husband-and-wife team Carole and Michael Raschella. I shook just holding those scripts. I was scared to death and ridiculously excited at the same time. I couldn't wait to read them, but I was afraid of what I might find, as well.

We were not encouraged to read any future scripts on the set while shooting the current episode. I presume this was because they wanted to keep our focus on what we were working on at the time, but in this case an exception must have been made. No one said anything to me as I started reading Part 1 before I even realized what I was doing. I had worried about how they would deal with the scarlet fever issue.

In the original series of books, Mary contracts scarlet fever and, as a direct consequence, loses her sight. In our script, Mary's eyesight is diminishing more and more until finally the doctor learns about the scarlet fever that she contracted when she was younger. He unfortunately has to give Pa the terrible news that, because the illness weakened the nerves in her eyes, she will certainly go blind.

This scene, where Charles gets the news about his fifteen-year-old daughter losing her sight, is powerful and tragic. Mike and Ford Rainey, who played Dr. Burke, were both outstanding. I defy anyone to watch either one of these episodes and not shed a tear. Most people need a bunch of Kleenex. I certainly teared up just reading them.

As I neared the end of Part 1, I could now see what Mike had been talking about the night of the wrap party. What an acting performance I would have to pull off to make this work! Again, those anticipatory, scared, excited feelings welled up.

I loved the scene where Mike sits in the church trying to understand why this terrible thing is happening. Reverend Alden tries to comfort Charles. He explains that God must have some special purpose in store for Mary.

Charles then says, "I have to tell my daughter that she is going blind. What should I tell her is that special purpose?"

Part 1 ends with Mary and Pa going off to Iowa to the school for the blind. Just reading it, I was already wrung out. I couldn't imagine the drama Part 2 had in store for me. It was a good thing I had to get back to work on the current show, because I really needed a break.

At the end of the day, in the car on the ride to my home in Toluca Lake, I dove into Part 2. It opens with Pa and Mary arriving at the school for the blind and Mary meeting her teacher, Adam Kendall, played by Linwood Boomer, who was around six feet tall, with thick brown hair and long eyelashes. He was handsome in a nontraditional way. Linwood was nervous, but it sure didn't show. He couldn't have been nicer or funnier with his oddball sense of humor. He would constantly say to me, "Your eyes are like two limpid pools shining in the moonlight," and I would always laugh. It's no surprise to me that he became a producer of *Night Court* and then created *Malcolm in the Middle.* He found his niche, and he has earned his success.

Portraying a blind person required a great deal of research, which I started soon after reading these scripts. I didn't want to be disrespectful or cartoonish. I was particularly proud of my blind gaze. I purposefully concentrated on not focusing my eyes on *anything,* so that literally anybody or anything could be moving around in my line of vision, so to speak, and it would have no effect on me whatsoever.

When I hear stories of actors behaving badly and flying into a rage when a crew member dares to flinch in that actor's eye line whilst he is emoting, I cringe. I learned well on *Little House*. We did not behave that way. I *was* proud that I could ignore distractions even while portraying someone who couldn't see.

As I read the script then and watch the episodes now, I am reminded of all the new things I had to learn to be able to pull this off. I visited the Foundation for the Junior Blind in Los Angeles and worked with teachers there. We also had one of the teachers come to the set for these two episodes in case any technical questions came up.

They told me that a blind person will typically shuffle her feet when she walks, until she learns how to use a cane (to know what obstacles might be in front of her). Understandable, when you think about it. If you really didn't know where you were going, you'd be walking very tentatively.

Also, they told me to use my outstretched arm in front of me to feel ahead for obstacles. Again, that wouldn't be necessary once one learned to use a cane. The cane taps the ground and moves from side to side in front of the user. When one leg steps forward, the cane is swept in front of the opposite leg, to check for obstacles before *that* foot steps out. In the blind school on *Little House*, we had chair rails along all of the walls so that the students could easily find their way around the hallways.

One scene early in Part 2 is particularly heartbreaking. Mary is told to unpack and is carefully shuffling around her room, feeling her way to a bureau for her clothes. As she puts her bag down, her hand grazes a mirror. How terrible for a teenage girl not to be able to look at herself in the mirror.

I learned that the eyes of someone who has recently lost their sight, but once was able to see, will appear more focused than the eyes of someone who is born blind. If the eyes have once learned to focus, they will often *appear* to be focused, even if they are unable to see. The teachers explained that that was why we so often see the blind wearing dark glasses; they may be self-conscious about how their eyes look. It's really our lack of understanding and lack of knowledge that makes us sometimes feel uncomfortable around people who happen to not be able to see.

The more I learned, the more I could open my mind and become more accepting and understanding of people with any kind of disability. We tend to be afraid of what we don't know, and I'm glad our show helped to dispel some of those feelings.

I learned that when a newly blind person sits in a chair, she will almost always sit on her hand. She wants to make sure that that chair seat is *there,* of course. I learned how to pour liquid into a cup by putting my index finger of one hand just over the edge and into the top of the cup or glass. That way, when you pour, you know when to stop.

We have a scene in Part 2 that shows Mary learning how to eat by using a "clock" system. Each food group is placed specifically on the plate at invisible "hours" of a clock. For example: the peas will be at three o'clock, while the meat might be at seven o'clock, etc. Pretty ingenious, I thought.

One thing I learned that was most helpful to me was that when I was playing "blind" Mary, I had to react to noises and voices in a completely new way. If I was playing "sighted" Mary, and I heard a crash to my right, I would snap my head toward that sound. But even before my head could turn, my eyes would be there first. Now that I was blind, my eyes would always *follow.* So, if someone across the room talked to me, my head would move, and my eyes would follow. This was probably the most difficult thing for me. It never got any easier. I always had to concentrate to do this, but I believe my hard work paid off. I really thought I looked convincing on screen.

I actually received many letters from people who thought that I, Melissa Anderson, had gone blind, and that the producers had written that into our show. Now, that's a compliment! I also received letters from blind people telling me what a good job I had done. They watched the show, and along with their sighted friends and relatives, critiqued my performance. How honored I felt to get these letters of endorsement.

I worked so hard perfecting this performance that I found myself acting "blind" during the first rehearsal of *The Love Boat,* which was my first time shooting something different since my character on *Little House* went blind. Luckily, no one else noticed.

We have scenes in Part 2 where you see Mary learn to write using a ruler to keep the lines straight and also learning to read Braille. I had to learn to look as if I had mastered reading and could do it using both hands. I practiced this a lot. Obviously, I couldn't really read Braille that fast, but I managed to make it look pretty good.

A poignant moment in this episode is when Mary finally realizes that her teacher, Adam, is also blind. She was so self-involved at first, and then working so hard to learn, that she just never stopped to think that her teacher might be just like her. When Adam asks her what *she* looks like, she realizes that he's never seen her, either. Awww. Really, so sweet.

Toward the end of the episode, Mary announces that she'll be going to Winoka, in Dakota Territory, with Adam to open a new school for the blind there. She and Adam have fallen in love, and Mary will be a teacher, just as she and Ma had always planned. Charles and Caroline decide to follow them to Winoka because times are so hard in Walnut Grove, and they feel that the family needs a new start.

In the final scene, Mary speaks to her church congregation at Walnut Grove and leads them in prayer, which she reads from her Braille Bible. I was surprised and happy to see that they froze the frame on my face at the very end. It was a really nice way to end this ultra dramatic two-part episode.

Mike was right, it *was* a great acting challenge for me, and I ate it up. I loved it.

The Neilsen Ratings for Part 1 put us at #2, and for Part 2, #1. We had never had ratings that high in our four-year history. I became the first and only actress in television history to portray a character who is struck with an affliction and never recovers. I was nominated for Outstanding Lead Actress in a Drama Series, the youngest actress ever to receive a nomination in this category. I was also the only actor from our show to receive a nomination in its entire eight-year run. I was invited to be one of the actors announcing the nominations that year, which you have to do at some ungodly hour of the morning, as the show goes live to the east coast at 8:00 a.m. It turned out to be worth it because that is how I found out about my *own* nomination. I was unbelievably excited and celebrated by going out to lunch at my favorite restaurant at that time, Sorrentino's, in Toluca Lake.

Technically I was in the wrong category. I was actually a "supporting" actor on the series; Mike and Karen were the "leads." In the 1977–78 awards season, the Television Academy asked us to submit one episode from that season to be considered and voted on by a jury of peers. I submitted "I'll Be Waving As You Drive Away" Part 1 (when Mary goes blind) for consideration. Because I was the featured actress in that particular episode, they deemed me a "Leading Actress" and placed me in that category. That has since been changed. Now, if you are a supporting actor, you remain in the supporting category. A much better system, and much easier to understand.

Melissa Sue Anderson

HAIR: Light Brown
EYES: Blue
BORN: Sept. 26, 1962.

Robert Nightsmann
PHOTOGRAPHY

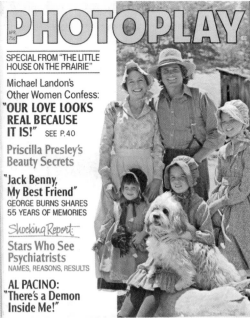

APR
75¢

PHOTOPLAY®

SPECIAL FROM "THE LITTLE
HOUSE ON THE PRAIRIE"

Michael Landon's
Other Women Confess:

"OUR LOVE LOOKS
REAL BECAUSE
IT IS!" SEE P.40

Priscilla Presley's
Beauty Secrets

"Jack Benny,
My Best Friend"
GEORGE BURNS SHARES
55 YEARS OF MEMORIES

Shocking Report:

Stars Who See
Psychiatrists
NAMES, REASONS, RESULTS

AL PACINO:
"There's a Demon
Inside Me!"

...e and my two best friends, Pam and Tam

Allan "Whitey" Snyder – makeup

The Landon family

The whole Michael Landon family turned up for the Concern Foundation's block party for the Cancer Fund in Beverly Hills. With Landon is wife Lynn, Mike Jr., 10, Leslie Ann, 12, and Shawna Leigh, 3.

Me on location shooting the pilot

Mitch Vogel and me

Victor French
"directing"

When I grow up,
Greg comes to my
wedding

Riding a horse with John

If looks could kill…

"Ain't no better piece of bottom land in this whole state."

"The Wisdom of Solomon"

LANCE KERWIN & Melissa Sue Anderson star in "James at 15," a new fall pilot and show on NBC! He's cute!

We were always a cute couple

'HECK, I'M JUST A COWBOY'

Landon—Father To Millions

By BARBRA ZUANICH
Herald-Examiner Staff Writer

The Paramount Studios sound stage was brimming with activity and energy.

It was one of those rare times that the setting of "Little House on the Prairie" ventured beyond rural Walnut Grove . . . this time to the city and a cotillion ball with music, young people, gala music and a dazzling Mary Ingalls and her father, Charles, descending a spiral staircase.

Scores of extras, dressed exquisitely for the occasion, waltzed to a turn-of-the-century melody.

Michael Landon, father figure of "Little House," walked his TV daughter down the steps to a waiting beau, and lingered, noting quietly how his little girl had grown, until the director announced "Cut."

After almost 20 consecutive seasons in front of TV cameras, (14 with "Bonanza") Landon is in the same long-standing league as Lucille Ball, Lawrence Welk and Walter Cronkite when it comes to sheer hours of performance. And his confidence on the set reflects the years of practice.

There is no strain, no trace of over-indulgence in the medium. Landon is renowned for creating a sense of calm among his co-workers; there may be behind-closed-doors disputes over content or dialogue, but never loud or lingering disagreements that disrupt work.

Landon seems almost too loose to be both star and executive producer (and sometimes writer AND director)

crew appreciates his relaxation.

Landon attributes his large dose of fatalism. "I anything," he says quietly. know how you'll be the c The outcome is totally de what's on opposite our sho up against a hot show, we know it. I refuse to get upset abou could panic, but it wouldn't says flatly.

A passing extra lightheart Landon why he hasn't wore the cotillion. "Heck, I'm j boy," joshes Landon. He casual, usually approachable

Even Landon's criterion as a soft-spoken observation an easy show to beat. It's can't show motorcycle cha wrecks. We've been written than once by the cynics read a review of a show aired. I believe many cr know much about the busi should get down on the set opportunity to understa they're writing about. So ma are so busy zinging the a never notice the script, the sets."

The conversation easily d Landon family — a whopp strong including dad and m "The kids vary in age from says Landon proudly. "And friends."

The brood includes two cl Landon's first marriage, a wife's first marriage, and h

Michael Landon with Melissa Sue Anderson, his daughter on "Little House on the Prairie". rs is an easy show to beat. It's soft. We can't w motorcycle chases or car wrecks."

"Times of Change"

"I'll Be Waving as You Drive Away"

"I'll Be Waving as You Drive Away" takes us to #1

Little House on Prairie Hits No. 1 for First Time

NBC's Little House on the Prairie, enjoying its best year in four seasons on the air, made it to the top of the ratings for the first time last week, according to figures released Tuesday by the A. C. Nielsen Co.

Little House, which had been in second place the week before with the first half of a two-part story about the eldest daughter becoming blind, moved into the No. 1 spot with the conclusion of that episode, topping ABC's perennial leaders of Laverne & Shirley and Three's Company which were ranked second and third, respectively.

All in the Family's season finale of last Sunday night, which brought the farewell of Mike and Gloria, was in fourth place. Rounding out the top 10 were (in order) Happy Days, The Waltons, Alice, MASH, 60 Minutes and Charlie's Angels.

The 11-20 programs were One Day at a Time, How the West Was Won, Soap, Love Boat, Police Story, Barney Miller, "It's the Easter Beagle, Charlie Brown," Incredible Hulk, Eight Is Enough and "The First Easter Rabbit."

Richie Brockelman, Private Eye placed 36th in its premiere, while Sam was 45th for its debut episode. Among special programming "Gene Kelly: An American in Pasadena" was 31st, the "AFI Salute to Henry Fonda" 37th and "Mysterious Castles of Clay" 42nd.

ABC won the week with an 18.8 rating and 30.8 share, with CBS a strong second posting an 18.3 rating and 30.3 share. NBC figures were 17.1 rating and 28.2 share. Season to date, it's ABC 20.9 rating and 33.8 share; CBS 18.8 rating and 30.3 share; NBC 18.0 rating and 29.1 share.

My 2-part "Going Blind" shows ranked #97

I am the youngest nominee

America's Foremost Casting Newspaper

The Hollywood DRAMA-LOGUE

NEW YORK, SAN FRANCISCO, LAS VEGAS

VOL. IX — NO. 40   HOLLYWOOD, CALIFORNIA, OCTOBER 6 — 12, 1978   PRICE 75 CENTS

AMERICAN FILM INSTITUTE OFFERS MANY OPPORTUNITIES FOR PARTICIPATION

BY JUNE AUGUST-SALOW

15th Annual Hugh O'Brian Acting Awards, Presented Oct. 12, Afford UCLA Students Showcase & Prizes

BY LEE MELVILLE

Hugh O'Brian. TV's *Wyatt Earp*. The names were synonymous for the six years the series ran over ABC. Even today, O'Brian is still more closely identified with the TV marshall than any

HUGH O'BRIAN

other character he has played. But it doesn't bother him; it never has. "That horse went to the bank every Friday,"

O'Brian states with an all-knowing smile. "It took me out of the feature player category at Universal and it gave me an opportunity to be in a position where today I have "go to hell" money — I don't have to do something unless I want to do it."

The legend of Wyatt Earp didn't stop after those first six years; the series has been in re-runs all over the world ever since. And it is that series that partially enables O'Brian to sponsor an annual acting awards program for UCLA theatre arts students.

Thursday, October 12 will be the date for the 15th Annual Hugh O'Brian Acting Awards, established by the actor in 1964. Since that time, UCLA undergraduates and graduates have been awarded a total of $32,500 in prize monies provided in perpetuity by O'Brian.

Meeting Hugh O'Brian at his plush offices on Wilshire Boulevard in Westwood, I find the same soft-spoken, strong-jawed, lean man who ruled the airwaves

(Continued on Page 13)

He said his name was Ed, here six months from Houston. We shared the spectacular view of Los Angeles from Greystone Park in Beverly Hills — the grounds surrounding AFI, the American Film Institute.

"I'm really getting to like California," he said. "Look. You can see the airport from here today. And the ocean."

(You should've been there; it was a rare smog-free day following Santa Ana winds.)

"Well, I did it!" He waited for me to ask what it was, so I did. "I submitted a proposal for an AFI grant," he said. "The Independent Filmmakers Program."

"What do you think your chances are?" I asked.

"I don't know. Not great. I hear there are 1000 applications for 35 grants."

"Congratulations for applying and good luck!" I meant it.

"Thanks. It sure would be a great opportunity."

Having just spoken with three staff members, I also had a picture of the American Film Institute as an opportunity — an opportunity for participation in the Institute's goals and programs. From Robert Blumofe, Director of AFI West, I got the sense of history — the commit-

ment to preserving America's film heritage and making it available to the public. From Jan Haag, who heads the Independent Filmmakers Program, the Directing

ROBERT BLUMOFE
Photo by Paul C. Babin

Workshop for Women, and the AFI/Motion Picture Academy Internship Program, I got a sense of the future of filmmaking. From Peter Bieler, General Manager, I got a sense of the present: the Center for Advanced Film Studies and the Master Seminar Series.

(Continued on Page 16)

EQUITY TO HALT RECIPROCAL INTER-UNION AGREEMENT

Actors Equity Association announced last week that as of April 1, 1979, it will no longer grant membership automatically to other talent union members. In a letter sent to all branches of its parent organization, the Associated Actors & Artistes of America, Equity's executive secretary Donald Gordy stated that Equity membership will be granted only to holders of bona fide Equity contracts or graduates from apprenticeship, as of that date.

The present policy, which was instituted by Equity in 1964, permits membership to Four A's members who have six months seniority in their respective unions and who apply for Equity membership.

Gordy said the reason behind Equity's decision "was taken in an effort to curb the swelling ranks of individuals joining Equity without benefit of contract, but through their affiliation in a sister union. Concern has mounted over the increasing number of new members who have neither experience nor knowledge in the professional theatre."

Four A's members will have a six-month grace period until April 1, in which they may join Equity without a contract.

Melissa Sue Anderson of 'Little House' Is Youngest Emmy Nominee

BY ELLEN FITZHUGH

Our booth at Musso and Frank's is rather full of ladies — there's Melissa Sue Anderson (Missy, as she prefers to be called); her mother, Marian; her publicity representative, Bonnie; my own teen-aged daughter, Shannon, and me. A kind of pleasant verbal free-for-all ensues, with Missy the composed and benign focus of the discussion.

Knowing that she had just returned from a tour of the South Seas, including Tahiti, Bora Bora and Hawaii, I ask Missy how she liked it. "Don't go there," she says. "Look at the post cards." The heat and humidity, it turns out, were insufferable, and on Bora Bora there's some kind of flea-like insect that ravages the legs of the natives and left Missy with several painful bites. It was not the ideal vacation. We move on to discussing happier topics.

Missy turned sixteen last month, the youngest age at which anyone has received an Emmy nomination for outstanding lead actress in a dramatic series. This recognition for her work as Mary Ingalls in *Little House on the Prairie* is only one of several outstanding achieve-

MELISSA SUE ANDERSON

ments. She may well hold the record for length of a close-up in a dramatic series.

This happened when Michael Landon, unavailable to do his close-ups in a scene with her, suggested she could carry the weight of the scene herself. And she did. For four minutes.

She's also the first regular in a series

(Continued on Page 13)

ACTORS' FUND BLOOD DRIVE OCT. 9

The 1978 Actors' Fund Blood Drive will be held on Columbus Day, Monday, October 9, at the Bob Hope U.S.O. Club, 1741 N. Ivar Street in Hollywood, from 11 AM to 5:30 PM.

Helen Hayes, Kelly Lange and Chris-tine Lund will head the drive, which now in its ninth year has become the largest such blood drive in the entire Los Angeles-Orange County area. Stars will act as hosts and hostesses while serving coffee and donuts to blood donors.

Theatre owners and producers of legitimate theatre attractions and other activities have donated over 750 pairs of gift tickets to such attractions as *Dracula*, *Annie*, *Sound of Music*, *Zoot Suit*, *Beatle-mania*, Universal Studios Tours, Disney-land and Magic Mountain.

Specific donor appointments can be made by calling The Fund at 464-4171, weekdays between the hours of 10 AM and 4 PM. This year's goal is 500 blood units which would reach the 1977 drive mark. All members of the entertainment industry are urged to attend, says the Fund's Western Region representative Ignatius J. (Iggie) Wolfington.

Such a pretty picture

Storm ends with wedding on prairie

By LINDA KING LAIRD

Laura Ingalls Wilder only mentioned her sister's blindness briefly in her famous Little House books.

Her fate has been dealt with in far greater detail, however, in Michael Landon's "Little House on the Prairie," NBC's top-rated weekly series.

Melissa Sue Anderson was just 11 when she began playing Mary, Laura's older sister. Now she's 16 and that has to say something about the show's success.

"Little House" began in September, 1974, starring then, as it does today, Anderson, Landon, Karen Grassle and Melissa Gilbert.

In the final episode of last season, Mary went blind and went off to a blind school. For the fifth season — the premiere was Sept. 18 — the Wilder family moved from the prairie to Winoka in the Dakota Territory. Charles (Landon) managed a hotel and his wife, Caroline (Grassle) cooked for the establishment.

The move was far from successful for Pa and Ma Ingalls and Mary has bid goodby to her family as they moved back to Walnut Grove.

This week, we find Mary, now teaching at the blind school, accepting the marriage proposal of Adam Kendall, the young man who taught her at the school. But Adam (Linwood Boomer) is also blind and Mary begins to have doubts as to whether two blind people can safely raise children and survive on the prairie.

"When he asks me, I say yes," said the pert, blond actress. "I've waited for this for a long time, but then I start thinking about having children. They were so important in those days. And I'm not sure about whether we can handle it."

Landon, who plays Pa and is also the executive producer and director, gave Mary a reason to resolve her doubts — a prairie dust storm.

"One of the blind children gets lost in the storm and Adam and I go out and look for her," she commented.

Anderson said being the only regular "blind" actress on television has been both "different and harder, but fun."

She was asked if she thought that a blind couple would have been able to manage 100 years ago as well as today. "Yeah, I think they could," she said, explaining that the wife of one of the men on the set has a cousin who is blind. "She's married to a blind man and she came out to the set and talked with me.

"She said, 'Truthfully, I think you're doing it well.'" Anderson reported. "She 'watches' television and her husband tells her how things are done. I think she understands well."

Anderson said the scripts for her have been written well. And she believes Mary and her future husband have not been made out to be super heroes in any way. Arthur Heinemann gets credit for writing this week's wedding episode.

Future episodes will see the Kendalls moving their school to Walnut Grove, where they will be reunited with the Ingalls clan.

Anderson said she doesn't or hasn't attempted to change the scripts in any way except in expression. "I'm free to add something in the way of expression but it's really not my end to tell them how to write. I'm the actress, not the writer."

Anderson would like to get into the directing or cinematography of television and has been learning from Landon (who learned himself on the set of "Bonanza"). She plans to take a few college courses in those subjects now that she's out of high

Linwood Boomer and Melissa Sue Anderson play Adam and Mary who marry on "Little House on the Prairie" at 7 p.m. Monday on 27 and 4.

THE NOMINATIONS

OUTSTANDING CONTINUING PERFORMANCE BY A SUPPORTING ACTOR IN A DRAMA SERIES
For a regular or limited series

OSSIE DAVIS
King .... NBC
WILL GEER
The Waltons .... CBS
ROBERT VAUGHN
Washington: Behind Closed Doors .... ABC
SAM WANAMAKER
Holocaust .... NBC
DAVID WARNER
Holocaust .... NBC

OUTSTANDING CONTINUING PERFORMANCE BY A SUPPORTING ACTRESS IN A DRAMA SERIES
For a regular or limited series

MEREDITH BAXTER BIRNEY
Family .... ABC
TOVAH FELDSHUH
Holocaust .... NBC
LINDA KELSEY
Lou Grant .... CBS
NANCY MARCHAND
Lou Grant .... CBS
KRISTY MC NICHOL
Family .... ABC

OUTSTANDING LEAD ACTRESS IN A DRAMA SERIES

MELISSA SUE ANDERSON
Little House On The Prairie .... NBC
FIONNULA FLANAGAN
How The West Was Won .... ABC
KATE JACKSON
Charlie's Angels .... ABC
MICHAEL LEARNED
The Waltons .... CBS
SUSAN SULLIVAN
Julie Farr, M.D. .... ABC
SADA THOMPSON
Family .... ABC

OUTSTANDING LEAD ACTOR IN A DRAMA SERIES

EDWARD ASNER
Lou Grant .... CBS
JAMES BRODERICK
Family .... ABC
PETER FALK
Columbo .... NBC
JAMES GARNER
Rockford Files .... NBC
JACK KLUGMAN
Quincy .... NBC
RALPH WAITE
The Waltons .... CBS

My Emmy doubles as grad cap stand

During a bizarre birthday party, Virginia Wainwright (Melissa Sue Anderson) confronts her anguished father (Lawrence Dane) and learns the truth of her own traumatic past in "Happy Birthday To Me." The psychological mystery, also starring Glenn Ford, is a Columbia Pictures release.

With Larry Dane and a knife!

One of my favorite photos

Barbara, Sinatra's look-alike son Frank Jr. (center), his date (second from left) actress Melissa Sue Anderson, and Sinatra's daughter Tina are all smiles for the big occasion.

Barbara, me, Frank Jr., Tina, & Frank Sinatra

Patti Davis, Jay Bernstein, me, and Tim Hutton

Look at that hair!

Funny "Julie Fenton," one of my favorite characters

Landon
and
Evigan
see
Melissa
Sue
Anderson's
dream day
come true

PHOTOS: IAN VAUGHN

Landon, with his wife Cindy, left, gives the bride a bit of last-minute fatherly advice.

My Two Dads star Greg Evigan bride happiness at the star-s

Michael Landon escorts Melissa Sue in her *Little House* wedding.

Little bride on the prairie

MICHAEL LANDON watched like a proud father as his *Little House on the Prairie* daughter Melissa Sue Anderson married Michael Sloan, creator of *The Equalizer*.

"It seemed Charles Ingalls was sitting there instead of Michael Landon," said one guest, referring to Landon's *Little House* character. "When he arrived, he looked more handsome than ever. His suit was dark, his face was tan and he wore sunglasses."

Melissa, 27, who played Mary on *Little House*, began dating Sloan, a 43-year-old Englishman, three years ago when she played the daughter of Edward Woodward's character McCall on *The Equalizer*.

After their wedding in Los Angeles, they left for a second ceremony in England, where another of Melissa Sue's on-screen fathers — Woodward — would see them exchange vows.

The star-studded St. Patrick's Day wedding was on the Garden Roof of the Bel-Age Hotel. Against the view of the Hollywood Hills shone such luminaries as Robert Wagner, Parker Stevenson and Kirstie Alley, Lindsay Wagner, Greg Evigan and Dennis Weaver. "When Michael Landon showed up with his wife Cindy, all eyes were upon them," said a guest.

The bride's real-life father James gave her away while Landon watched happily.

"Melissa was like a dream out of an 18th-century novel in her flowing gown of creamy silk," said the guest.

Cheers actor Roger Rees, who plays the millionaire beau of Kirstie Alley's character, was an usher. Among the 100 guests were celebrities Doug McClure, Robert Vaughn, David McCallum, Richard Anderson, Patrick Macnee, Rory Calhoun and George Lazenby. Robert DeLaurentiis was best man. ☐

Melissa Sue Anderson, 27, and Michael Sloan, 43, met when she guest-starred on his

This hangs in my hallway at home

Where does the time go… ?

SEASON FIVE
May 1978–January 1979

CHAPTER SIXTEEN

"The Wedding," the Emmys, and *Cooking?* with Steven Spielberg

"The Wedding" was another episode finely written by Arthur Heinemann but directed by Mike this time. We all worked very hard in difficult circumstances to make this episode and were rewarded by a number one rating for only the second time in our history.

It begins with Adam nervously rehearsing his marriage proposal. Okay. He thinks he's ready. Off he goes. Knocks on my door and says,

"Mary, I want you to hear me out without any interruptions."

"Certainly," I reply.

"I have to go to the Post Office. I'll be right back."

He leaves, walks down the hall, thinks twice; decides he'll try again.

Knock. Knock.

He comes back in and says, "The school's getting way too crowded, and I think you should give up your room."

"And go where?" I ask.

"Into my room?"

This isn't coming out the way he planned and I don't find it funny. Adam tells me it's not supposed to be funny, it's supposed to be a proposal.

"That's the most ridiculous proposal I've ever heard."

But, of course, I'm thrilled to accept.

We cut to the exterior of the Little House and barn where Charles comes screaming down the hill in the wagon. He pulls up in the yard with the telegram I've sent.

Caroline reads it and says, tearfully, "Mary's getting married."

Charles can't afford for the whole family to make the trip to Winoka for my wedding, so Laura and Albert, the Ingalls's adopted son, will look after their younger siblings. Albert was played by Matthew Labyorteaux, a fine young actor who had caught Mike's attention in our third season when he portrayed Charles as a young boy.

Nels Oleson gives Charles a lovely wedding gift for us. It is an ornate box with a tiny chirping bird that sings when you open it. He cautions Charles not to tell *Mrs.* Oleson, though.

The Reverend Alden will be on the road preaching around the time of my wedding. He wants to officiate, if there's any way he can get there. He doesn't want to miss it. Caroline is so ecstatic she kisses him! The Reverend asks Charles and Caroline not to tell Mary—just in case. He wouldn't want me to be disappointed. They tell him they won't say a word; it'll be a surprise.

Charles and Caroline are on the train preparing to leave, except that Caroline is having great difficulty saying goodbye to the kids.

I've been there.

Charles chides, "Caroline, would you let the children get off the train before it leaves?"

We see the train chugging away.

Charles and Caroline have arrived in Winoka, which, by the way, was shot on the Warner Bros. Western Street. We really got around! They are taking the stage to meet us. Adam and I are standing outside waiting for them. They see us and yell, and I wave to them in anticipation.

When they finally arrive, Ma says, "Oh, Mary, you look just beautiful. You, too, Adam."

She's a tad overexcited, I'd say.

After they have had time to unpack and rest up a bit, we all get together over sandwiches and talk. The subject of children comes up.

Ma and Pa are recounting stories of my mischievous childhood for Adam. We can tell by the look on my face that something isn't right. I tell everyone that I'm tired.

"All the excitement, I guess," I say as I start off to my room. As I walk, I am replaying their words in my mind. "She was the fastest runner. One second she'd be there, then I'd turn around, she'd be half a mile down the road."

That night, Caroline tells Charles, "Something's bothering Mary."

"Well, whatever it is, I'm sure she'll come to you with it. She always has."

The next day Charles goes to see the Reverend Corliss of Winoka, who is expecting to officiate at my wedding. We presume Charles lets him in on the Reverend Alden secret. The Reverend Corliss character was played by the late Louis Fant, a famous interpreter for the deaf. Not a bad actor, either.

Ma comes to the School for the Blind to see me. She gives me her beautiful blue wedding dress.

I cry.

"Mary, what's wrong?"

I fall apart.

Then I say, "Ma, I'm afraid."

"Are you nervous about the wedding? Most people usually are."

"No."

Ma says, "Then what is it?"

"It's hard to explain."

"Have you talked to Adam about it?' she asks.

I respond, "I don't want to hurt him."

Ma patiently asks, "How can talking out your problems with someone you love hurt them?"

I tell her she's right. "I'll talk to him tonight."

Later, Adam is talking as he enters my room. When I don't respond, he says, "Mary?"

Beat. Then, "I'm here, Adam."

He doesn't understand why I didn't answer him, and he kids me about having second thoughts.

"Why, Mary, you'd have to be blind not to want to marry a man like me."

Cute.

"You didn't know I was in the room, did you?" I ask, pointedly.

He doesn't know what that has to do with anything.

"If we had a child and that child wandered away or got into trouble . . ."

I could go on and on.

Adam says, "We've got more than twenty here at the school, and we handle them alright."

"They're blind, too. They're not gonna just wander off by themselves," I reply tersely.

"Mary, I *know* it's not going to be easy."

And I blurt out, "I don't want to marry you."

Poor Adam is having trouble taking all of this in. Linwood does a great job in this scene.

He can only manage, "Let's talk about this tomorrow."

"This *is* tomorrow."

Mean.

Adam walks over to the door. Opens it and slams it shut again. He paces up and down. Clearly he is distraught. He loses it.

"All parents ever pray for when they have a child is that it be healthy. And we can't have a child because God might give us a healthy one? Maybe we should just pray to God and ask him for a blind baby so we can take care of it and not have to worry about it."

Adam is emotionally exhausted. He tells me not to break the news to the children until after the picnic they are planning for us. He leaves. In Charles and Caroline's hotel room, there is a knock on the door. Charles answers it, and Adam almost falls inside. He is heartbroken.

It's picnic day, and the children from the blind school are having a great time. They are so happy for us. Charles is playing the . . . harmonica? I didn't know he was multi-talented. Caroline, Adam, and I are all miserable.

Charles and Caroline talk about me and my problems. They wish they could do something to help the situation. Suddenly we hear a loud noise. Cattle are being herded to safety by a man on horseback who yells that a dust storm, a bad one, is coming.

"Head for cover!"

The wind is blowing up a storm—literally. Dust, dirt, and debris are flying everywhere. Charles and Caroline help us get all of the blind children inside safely, but we discover that Susan Goodspeed is missing. Adam goes back out immediately. I follow. Ma takes my hand and is suddenly hit hard with some flying debris. She falls to the ground.

I scream "Ma" and Adam yells for someone to carry the wounded Caroline back into the school.

I insist on going with Adam to look for the missing child, saying, "The children are my responsibility, too."

We make our way as best we can in this terrible wind, dirt flying into our eyes.

Defeated, I yell, "Adam, we'll never find her."

But he yells back resolutely, "Yes, we will. Now, that's the difference between us. If there's something I have to do, I *do* it. I don't just give up."

Good for him. Mary's competitive spirit has kicked into gear.

"Neither do I."

At this point in the story, I must tell you that shooting in a simulated dust storm is unbelievably miserable. Huge Ritter fans blew gale-force winds at us while special effects people emptied bags of Fuller's Earth in front of them. We had grimy, sticky silt stuck to every inch of us. I would jump in the shower as soon as I got home on those days. I'd be in there forever, trying to wash all of that dirt out of my hair! The worst part was that even after all of that washing and scrubbing, I'd still have to get up the next morning at the crack of dawn, no, *before* the crack of dawn, to (lightly) wash my hair all over again, so that our hair stylist would be able to style it for that day. This went on for the four days that we shot that dust storm. Believe me, all of us were glad when it was finished!

Anyway, back in the thick of it, Adam and I are screaming, "Susan! Susan!"

Charles has gone out after us: "Adam! Mary!"

Adam and I think we hear something. A voice? Then, faintly, "I'm here." And then louder, "I'm here!"

We find Susan. She is scared crazy. She can't stop screaming, "I'm here!"

I say, "We knew we had to find you and we did. All a body has to do is set their mind to something, and then do it."

Adam is relieved to know that his old Mary is back.

Susan is still crying, and I say, more forcefully, "You're all right. We found you."

She finally starts to calm down, and I ask her, "How'd you like to be the flower girl at my wedding?"

Adam grins. We smooch.

Happily ever after.

Except Charles is still out there, screaming for us.

Finally, we hear him and he hears us and he figures out where we are. When he sees us, we are still smooching. He smiles and says, "I take it everything's all right!"

We all laugh.

Finally, it is the big day. It doesn't look like Reverend Alden will make it after all. At least I didn't know about it, so I won't be disappointed. Pa walks me down the hallway and to the scene of my wedding. The room is beautiful—awash with light. The colors are muted, there is fine dust in the air, and there is pretty, soft lighting.

As Reverend Corliss begins the ceremony, he sees a grimy-faced Reverend Alden step into the room. They nod to each other, secretively. Reverend Alden takes over from Reverend Corliss seamlessly. I hear his voice and break into a bigger grin. What a great surprise!

Adam and I recite our vows.

I notice as I watch this today that I am trying to hide my ever-growing fingernails from the camera as he slips the ring on. I was trying desperately to keep my nails nice so they would look pretty for the upcoming Emmy Awards, but let's face it: Blind pioneers didn't have long nails. Mike and Co. were nice about this, and they let it go. And as I watch it now, they're not quite as bad as I remember.

Back to Reverend Alden, who says, "And whom God hath joined together, let no man put asunder."

We tell each other, "I love you." The camera freezes on our smooch.

I was excited about Emmy night and decided to wear a beautiful steel-blue-colored dress that was designed for me. One of our makeup men, Hank Edds, came to my home to do my makeup. That was a first for me. I had my nails done, as well.

One day on the set, Mike said to me, "You know you're not going to win."

Did I mention Mike's mean streak?

"Oh, yeah, I know, I'm sure I won't." Still, his words kind of stopped me in my tracks.

"The deal is that one year a West Coast Screen Actors Guild performer wins, and the next year a member from the East Coast side of the Guild. That's my theory."

I was hopeful, but I was realistic. Most likely I was not going to win, but not for the reason he stated. I could not imagine myself winning against the other five wonderfully talented adult women I was in the category with: Fionnula Flanagan, Kate Jackson, Michael Learned (whom I knew personally and really liked), Susan Sullivan, and Sada Thompson.

That Emmy ceremony seemed interminably long while awaiting my category. I couldn't help thinking that I would be an absolute wreck if I *did* win and had to walk up onto that stage. I have horrible stage fright when I'm just myself and not portraying a character.

In the end, Mike was right again, as Sada Thompson, a New York actress, won. I could actually breathe, now that I knew. I could enjoy the rest of the show—which now flew by. They always say that it's an honor just to be nominated, and honestly I believe that to be true. After the awards ceremony, I went to Sorrentino's again and ordered my favorite dinner: salad with Green Goddess dressing and lobster. It was a once-in-a-lifetime experience that I will always remember.

Little House had never been an industry-watched show, but with the hype that accompanied these highly rated episodes, that perception changed. In this very short span of time, my profile went from low to high, from kind of interesting to pretty exciting.

During my hiatus in 1979, I appeared in some very diverse and interesting projects. *The Survival of Dana* was a CBS TV movie co-starring Robert Carradine. It was about a young girl (me) coming from Fargo, North Dakota, to live with her grandmother in Los Angeles. The grandmother was played by Marian Ross of *Happy Days* wearing a gray wig. Dana experiences major culture shock as she tries to fit in with all of the new kids she meets and doesn't always make the best decisions. I had a great time making this movie because I got to be the "bad" girl in it, at least for a while. Bobby Carradine was about twenty-four when we shot this. He was already a dad—to an adorable daughter, Ever, who is now an actress, as well.

Next came *Which Mother Is Mine?* for ABC and Martin Tahse Productions once again. Interestingly, I worked with Marian Ross again here. This time she played my foster mother. That's an actress for you. She wasn't so vain to think that she couldn't play a grandmother, and then turned right around to play a mother more her own age. Working with her was always a pleasure. I earned my second Emmy nomination for that program.

Toward the end of my break, I got an offer from Aaron Spelling to do another episode of *The Love Boat*. I always liked working for Aaron, and the script for this was cute. It was a Halloween episode, and I was to play a pseudo Cinderella character. The only catch was that my Cindy character had to sing. Sing? Me?? Uh, I am not exactly known for my singing ability. I got nervous just thinking about it. But I mustered up my courage; I would conquer my fear. I agreed to act in this episode and . . . sing in it, too.

The producers let me know that I would be singing "Witchcraft." Oh. That's nice. What was that? I'd never heard of that song before. My mother knew, though.

"Oh, yes, Frank Sinatra recorded it; it was a big hit in the late fifties."

So I get the album *Sinatra's Sinatra* and listen to this song. This is *not* going to be easy. It's kind of tricky rhythmically, and my pitch? Well . . . did I mention what a competent actress I am? But I practiced, and I practiced. I tried. Hard.

The producers told me that I had to go to the recording studio to pre-record my song. Huh? Did they say pre-record? Oh, what had I gotten myself into?

I dressed in my favorite new outfit, hoping that it would bring me luck: a boat-necked shirt in a pretty shade of purple with purple pin-stripe pants and pretty matching purple pumps. Believe it or not, it looked good. Maybe if I looked good, they would think I *sounded* good, too.

I arrived at the recording studio at the appointed time, and we got right down to it. It was all so professional—me in the little sound-proof booth, the music production team with their big mixing board in their own medium-sized room, and real live musicians in the bigger room.

The ambience was great. Dark and dramatic, as if I were a real singer! Recording a real song! Oh, I cannot tell you how nervous I was inside my little air-conditioned booth, dripping with sweat.

We rehearsed. The producer would say, "Okay, this is a rehearsal. 'Witchcraft,' and here we go."

I'd sing my heart out, and he would give me notes. One more rehearsal. I sang again. More notes.

The producer said, "Let's put one down, this time. Here we go, Melissa. This is 'Witchcraft,' take one."

I sang.

> Those fingers in my hair.
> That sly, come-hither stare
> That strips my conscience bare;
> It's Witchcraft.

Not *so* bad. On I went.

> And I've got . . .

I'm out of tune. I try again.

"'Witchcraft,' take two."

I hear my voice in the headphones singing:

> Those fingers in my hair.
> That slyyyy come-hither stare
> That strips my conscience bare
> It's Witchcraft.

Then I sing,

> And I've got noooo defense for it.
> The heat is tooo intense for it.
> What good would common sense for it doooo?

"Okay," says the producer. "Not bad, Melissa. Remember to watch your pitch. I know it's a difficult song, but you're doing o-kay, so far. Let's move along to the bridge."

Ugh, I thought. I'm ready to *die* in here. I took a deep breath. "'Witchcraft,' take three."

I hear my voice in the headphones, once again. I jump in at,

'Cause it's Witchcraft, wicked Witchcraft
And although I know it's strictly taboooo . . .

"Lost your pitch, Melissa. Let's go again."

"Right," I say.

I swear, I lost ten pounds doing this—between the nerves and the sweat. I go again. Better. Not great. On to, "'Witchcraft,' take five."

When you arouse the need in me
My heart says yes indeed in me.
Proceed with what you're leading me tooooo.
It's such an ancient pitch
But one I wouldn't switch.
'Cause there's no nicer witch than you.

"And, not bad, Melissa. Let's get that big finale with this one. 'Witchcraft,' take six."

Here I go again, I think. If I can just manage to get this ending, I'll have done it. Please, God, please!

It's such an ancient pitch
But one I'd never switch.
'Cause there's no nicer witch than youuuuuuuuuuuu.

"We got it, Melissa. Good job. That's a wrap for you."

Never mind that my cute purple outfit was soaked in sweat.

"Thanks for all your help," I say, relieved, and I *meant* it.

I reported to the *Love Boat* set at Twentieth Century Fox on that following Monday morning to shoot the "Cindy" episode. I had two stepsisters and a wicked stepmother, played by Carolyn Jones of *The

Adams Family. We had lots of fun shooting this, particularly when we all got dressed up for the Halloween Ball.

Frank Sinatra Jr. played Prince Charming, and ran around (in tights!) trying to find his Cinderella. I believe he says something like, "She looks like an angel, she sings like a nightingale . . ."

He *must* be kidding!

Anyway, he eventually catches up with me and, well, you know, we go on to live (and sing, I guess) happily ever after.

When I met Frank Jr. on the set, he was very nice. He was very complimentary about my version of his dad's song, too. On this *Love Boat* he sang, "Once Upon A Time," and I thought, boy, can *he* sing. He was a competent actor, but a fantastic singer. I always thought it was such a shame that he wasn't able to achieve the kind of success he deserved. Talk about living in the shadow of . . .

We became friends at that time but did not start actually dating until two years later. Good thing, since I was just sixteen when we met—what a scandal *that* would have been.

Frank invited me to be part of his group of friends who got together to watch movies that he would screen at his home. I met John Alonzo, the late Oscar-winning cinematographer, as well as William (Billy) Farrington, a homicide investigator for the Los Angeles Sheriff's Department. As you can see, Frank had a diverse bunch of friends.

I became good friends with Billy and his wife, Sylvia, and maintained that friendship for many years after Frank and I stopped dating. Billy was full of fascinating stories. He had worked on the Charles Manson case, even losing part of a finger in an accident during that investigation. It was nice to get to know people outside of show business—with very different careers and aspirations than I had.

After I'd known Frank for a while, he mentioned that his father would be doing some concerts and would I like to invite anyone to go to one of them? I immediately thought of my good friend Teri

Trescony. She was one of the daughters of Al Trescony from NBC. I had become close friends with their family during my years on *Little House,* and we still keep in touch. To say Teri Trescony was thrilled would be an understatement. She *adored* Frank Sinatra and simply could not imagine going to one of his concerts and getting to meet him.

We went to the concert which was, of course, outstanding and met Frank Sr. as well. I actually do not remember if this was *my* first meeting with him or if we'd met previously, but he was as kind and gracious as ever, and Teri had lived one of her dreams, to boot.

Frank Jr.'s family is a great bunch. His mother, Nancy, is a little dynamo, and what a cook! The story goes that Frank Sr. used to ask his ex-wife Nancy to make some of his favorite dishes for him and have them sent to his home, unbeknownst to his current wife! Tina was most like their father—passionate and headstrong. And Nancy was soft-spoken and very sweet. I had the pleasure of spending some nice evenings—not to mention great dinners—with them, and Tina and I share a good friend and great hair stylist, Eric Serena.

I visited the Frank Sinatra compound in Palm Springs before it was sold, attending parties and family get-togethers. It was a magnificent piece of property. The main house was one building. There were several guest bungalows, another large home, and two swimming pools as well as the movie theater, gym, and even a building for Frank's model trains.

I was lucky enough to meet Sammy Davis Jr. before he passed away. He and his wife, Altovise, were one of the nicest and most genteel couples I have ever met. I had always been such a fan of Sammy's, and I couldn't believe it when he said that *he* was a fan of mine.

I also met Kirk Douglas one evening, before he had his stroke. He had had a fair bit to drink and gave me his dissertation on acting. He expounded on the merits of the "Theatre." On and on he went, but that was okay with me. This was Kirk Douglas, for God's sake. Pretty cool. And it helped me make the decision to go to the Burt Reynolds Dinner Theater in Florida to act in Neil Simon's *The Gingerbread Lady* there.

On one of these Palm Springs occasions, I started looking through Frank Sr.'s leatherbound collection of his movie scripts. *From Here To Eternity, Pal Joey, The Manchurian Candidate, Man With The Golden Arm.* I picked out *Man With The Golden Arm* and started looking through it.

Up walked Frank Sr., saying, "Which one ya got there?"

I smiled and said, "Well, this one is my favorite, Frank. I thought your performance was amazing, and what a controversial topic for its time."

Frank replied, "Well, thanks for that, Missy. I'm kinda proud of that one."

On some of these nights before I went to sleep, I would think about some of these once-in-a-lifetime meetings and conversations that I'd had. I thought how lucky I was to have these experiences and how I knew that I'd always remember these special times.

My agent had been working with our *Little House* production staff to arrange for me to get a couple of hours off from work so that I might have the opportunity to meet with Steven Spielberg. He apparently wanted to talk to me about one of his upcoming projects, but he did not usually divulge what he was working on until *after* he had decided upon who would be part of his cast.

Little House was making things very difficult. They didn't *have* to let me off, and they wanted to make sure that I was aware of that. Ultimately this decision was Mike's, and it really didn't look good for a while there. Finally, an arrangement was worked out so that I'd be able to go and have the meeting, but Mike made sure to tell me how difficult it had been to rearrange the shooting schedule. He acted almost surprised that it meant so much to me. I thanked him, anyway, for the trouble and excitedly made plans to meet with Mr. Spielberg.

Oh, what to wear? What *do* you wear to a meeting you know nothing about? My agent had warned me that Steven liked to *do* things during meetings. He'd heard of him playing arcade games, going for target practice, and even cooking. That only complicated the matter. What do you wear to look like a character you know nothing about in a film you know nothing about and that won't seem ridiculous if you end up shooting at something?

Decisions. Decisions. And, left in the hands of a sixteen-year-old girl, a long and arduous task.

I finally decided on . . . wait for it . . . my purple (fitted) overalls with a bright pink shirt and platform shoes. That way, I thought, I was ready for anything.

I finished my work on *Little House* on the appointed day and quickly changed out of my 1870s clothes and into my 1970s clothes. I moderned up my hair and makeup and headed over to the Universal Studios lot where Steven Spielberg's Amblin Entertainment was housed.

EXT. UNIVERSAL STUDIOS GUARD GATE — DAY

A bright red Mustang pulls up, idles. A UNIVERSAL STUDIOS GUARD known to all as "Scotty," walks out of the guard hut to the driver's window.

                    SCOTTY
        Hi. May I help you?

                    MELISSA
        Oh, hi, Scotty. I'm Melissa Sue
        Anderson, and I'm here to meet with
        Steven Spielberg.

CONTINUED:

The GUARD looks down at his clipboard full of
appointments.

                    SCOTTY
          Yes, here we are. Let me give you a
          map and you can drive on over there.

                    MELISSA
          Thanks.

Scotty puts a "Visitor's Pass" inside the wind-
shield and hands Melissa a map. The barrier is
raised and the Mustang drives through.

AERIAL SHOT — TRAVELING — DAY

Of that red Mustang slowly driving through the
little alleyways between the soundstages of the
Universal lot.

EXT. AMBLIN BUILDING — DAY

The car comes to a stop in a Visitor's Parking
space opposite the Amblin building. Melissa EXITS
the car and walks into the building.

INT. AMBLIN BUILDING — RECEPTION AREA — DAY

Melissa approaches a RECEPTIONIST.

                    RECEPTIONIST
          May I help you?
                    (then, looking up)
          Oh, you're Melissa. Come right this
          way.

                    MELISSA
          Thank you.

CONTINUED:

CAMERA KEEPS WITH THEM as Melissa is led down
the hallway to a large room in the back of the
building.

INT. KITCHEN — DAY

STEVEN SPIELBERG is at the counter preparing what looks to be the ingredients for carrot
cake. He sees Melissa ENTER and walks over, hand
outstretched.

>   STEVEN SPIELBERG
> Hi, Melissa. I'm Steven. It's nice to
> meet you.

>   MELISSA
> Hi, Mr. Spielberg — Steven. It's my
> pleasure. I'm such a fan of your
> movies.
>   (beat)
> So, uh, what are you making here?
> Looks like carrot cake?

>   STEVEN SPIELBERG
> Yep.

He finishes grating the carrots and proceeds to
chop walnuts.

Beat, then:

>   MELISSA
> Uh, do you want some help?

>   STEVEN SPIELBERG
> Sure, Melissa. Can you start mixing up
> this batter?

CONTINUED:

                    MELISSA
   Okay.

Melissa starts mixing, wondering what to say next.
Finally:

                    MELISSA
   I bake a lot at home. I'm pretty good
   at desserts. I don't know how to
   make any regular stuff, though, like
   entrees. Just desserts.

             STEVEN SPIELBERG
        (busy finishing his chopping)
   That's kind of the way I am, too.

There is an awkward silence. Then:

             STEVEN SPIELBERG
   What's it like working with Michael
   Landon?

He has finally said something she can comment on.

                    MELISSA
       (relieved)
   Well, he's a pro. He knows what he
   wants. He doesn't waste time. And he's
   nice, too.

             STEVEN SPIELBERG
   Uh huh. Well, that's good.

Another long pause.

The cake batter has been poured into the pans and
Steven puts them into the oven.

             STEVEN SPIELBERG
   Want to make the frosting?

CONTINUED:

MELISSA
Sure.

On it went, awkward silences and all. I couldn't stay to see how it all turned out, but the cake really did look like it was going to be good. Now I knew why he liked to take meetings while otherwise occupied. He was really shy. The only thing he probably didn't count on was: so was I.

By the way, I later found out that the role I was being considered for was Marion in *Raiders of the Lost Ark*. They obviously decided to go "older" and hired actress Karen Allen, who was terrific in the part.

SEASON SIX
May 1979–January 1980

CHAPTER SEVENTEEN

I Was a Blind Pioneer and You Thought You Had Problems

Our kindly camera operator, Kenneth Hunter, came up with the story for "The Third Miracle" and received a "story by" credit. Kenny was one of the nicest people I've ever met. He must have been a great father because he was patient beyond belief. He was terrific at his job behind the camera, and we were all pleased to see his story come to fruition.

Mike directed this episode, which opens on an angry swarm of bees on a log near the Little House. *Too* near, if you ask me. This is Laura and Albert's latest business venture—making honey. They collect it and deliver it and rake in the money, honey. I mean, the honey money. They discuss what they will buy with their share. Laura wishes to impress Almanzo with a new outfit from head to toe. Albert wants a velocipede!

While she is in town, Caroline overhears Nellie scream at customers of her restaurant, "Get out!" if they're unsatisfied with her cooking. "And don't come back!"

Mrs. Foster sees Caroline and gives her a telegram for Adam.

Adam and I are smooching, once again, when Caroline arrives with the telegram. She reads it to us. Adam has been chosen to receive the Louis Braille Award for Dedicated and Distinguished Teaching. He is the first blind teacher ever to be so honored. The Awards Ceremony will be held in Saint Paul the next Saturday.

Adam questions how they even knew about him. I say that Hester-Sue (who had joined our show midway through Season Five and was played by Ketty Lester) and I nominated him.

"Thank you both very much. It's a wonderful honor. Lord knows, it's the second-best thing that ever happened to me, after Mary."

Awww.

But we don't have anywhere near enough money to afford the trip, so Adam is not going to be able to accept. Hester-Sue offers to give us the four dollars she has saved, and Adam and I have about twelve. He politely declines her offer.

Caroline says she'll talk to Charles, and when Adam protests, she says, "Adam, you're going to have to learn not to argue with your mother-in-law." She smiles.

Charles and Caroline discuss their trip at the dinner table.

"Caroline, I'd do anything to help them, you know that. But we don't have it, either. At least not that kind of money. Fifty or sixty dollars—there's no way I can swing it."

Laura and Albert exchange looks.

Cut to the interior of the loft that night. Laura and Albert are talking about it.

She says, "I'm willing."

And so is he.

They go downstairs to let Ma and Pa in on their plan.

Laura and Albert explain that Mr. Oleson made a deal to buy their honey for a total of fifty-seven dollars and sixty cents.

Laura says, "We decided to give it to Adam so he and Mary can go to St. Paul."

"You two worked a long time for that money," Pa says.

"We want to do it, Pa," Laura replies.

But Albert, always a realist, says, "'Cept you better know now, come Christmas, we won't be able to give you much of anything."

Caroline says, "Doing this for Mary and Adam is the best present you could have given us."

Charles and Caroline and Laura and Albert want to tell us the news right away.

Hester-Sue starts down the stairs muttering about whoever could be banging on the door in the middle of the night. Adam and I come to the stairs thinking that something must be wrong.

Caroline is ready to explode. "We have good news! We just couldn't wait!"

Laura proudly announces, "You and Adam are goin' on that trip."

I ask, "What?"

"Just consider it an early Christmas present from me and Albert."

We are thrilled and surprised. Yes, of course we want to go. Laura and I hug as only sisters can.

Laura and Albert go to Oleson's Mercantile to sell their honey. It seems that Mr. Oleson is away on a buying trip, so Mrs. O. is playing hardball. Even after hearing that this honey money will be given to us for our special trip, she will only give the kids half as much as her husband would have paid.

"Take it or leave it," she says.

Obnoxious.

Albert thinks fast and comes up with a plan.

He says, "Can't beat a good business woman like Mrs. Oleson." They will have to sell her their "main hive" so they can make up the rest of the money. "We were going to make a fortune off it." Albert is beating Mrs. Oleson at her own game. "It produces hundreds of pounds a year. It's breakin' my heart to give it up."

The wheels are turning in Mrs. Oleson's mean little mind. She thinks that hive could keep Nellie's Restaurant in sweets forever and says, "You've got a deal."

Albert tells Mrs. O. that she and Nellie will have to come out to the house to pick up the hive, as he only has the use of his Pa's wagon for today.

Mrs. Oleson agrees, but wonders if it might be dangerous.

Albert responds, "Oh, heck no. They're practically tame. 'Sides, if you pick them up *after* sun up, they'll all be takin' their morning naps."

That's good enough for Mrs. O., and she generously rounds that fifty-seven-sixty up to an even fifty-*eight*.

That's big of her.

Outside the store, Laura asks Albert, "How come you told her after sun up? It'll be hot then and the bees'll . . ."

Albert smiles slyly. "That's why *I'm* the genius."

We cut to the angry bees—for emphasis.

It is night and Adam lies awake. He gets out of bed and paces the floor. I awaken. He is worried; he does not like making speeches.

I tell him, "You're the first blind teacher to ever receive the award. I think you should make that an important part of your speech." I talk about when I got my first pair of glasses. "The kids called me 'Four Eyes,' and I thought that was just about the worst problem that could happen to me."

Adam thinks he gets it. "And that just proves that everything's relative. You learn to deal with these things, big or small, and you come out the stronger for it."

He likes my idea so much, he wants *me* to give his speech. Adam asks if I still have those eyeglasses.

I say, "Yeah, I think Ma has 'em. Why?"

"You could hold them up to illustrate your point when you make the speech."

Ha.

Unfortunately, the stagecoach that we must take to meet the train is badly in need of repairs. The driver says that the owners " . . . run these things right into the ground. Profits first. Repairs later."

We say goodbye. Ma hands me my glasses—because Adam said I wanted them.

Ha. Ha.

Sharing the stagecoach with us is Marge Lauren, a very pregnant young woman on her way to reunite with her husband in Minneapolis. Marge was played by Leslie Landon, who did a fine job in this role.

Back at the Little House, Nellie and Mrs. Oleson have come to collect their hive. They pick up the big log and carry it to their wagon, load it on, and ride off. As they ride, those angry bees start flying. They buzz and fly right around Mrs. O. and Nellie. They scream in terror!

On our stagecoach, the ride is extremely bumpy, and it seems that we now have an axle problem. The driver says, "I'm gonna have to take a detour in the nearest town and get it fixed."

Meanwhile, Marge offers us sandwiches, which we happily accept.

Cut to the exterior of the Sonora countryside as the stage rides along. The camera pushes in slowly to reveal that the pin that attaches the horses to the coach is bobbing up and down, obviously loose. The pin comes out; the horses go one way and the coach goes the other. It falls off the side of the road, flipping over and over down a mountainside. We can hear our screams from inside. The coach finally comes to rest on its side, far below.

I manage to sit up; I am not hurt, just banged up. I yell for Adam. He has been thrown outside of the coach.

I climb up and outside the coach and make my way to him.

He says, "My legs are pinned under the coach. I think they're broken."

I pull and pull but cannot lift the heavy coach.

Adam says, "Is Marge all right?"

I respond, "She's alive."

The driver doesn't seem to be so lucky. He was thrown far from the coach and looks to be dead.

In Walnut Grove, Mrs. Foster at the telegraph office runs to tell Charles that the stage is way overdue. Charles thinks it's that wobbly wheel and "they're probably stuck on the road somewhere." He and Garvey will take the wagon and pick us up.

Meanwhile, I've found the canteen and give Adam some water.

"They're not going to find us, Mary."

"Sure, they will," I say, mustering up false bravado.

"It would take a miracle. We're off the main route; they don't know what road we took. I can't feel my legs anymore," Adam says.

"My baby!" Marge screams from inside the overturned coach. She says that her water broke; we must get help. She cries, "I can't move."

I decide to go for help.

Adam says, "You can't."

"Adam, I'm the only one that can." I tell him, "I can feel the sun on my face. It's west of us. I'm gonna head north, back to the main road."

All I can say is, it's a good thing Mary seems to have a better sense of direction than I do on foot. *I'd* never find my way out.

Adam protests, but I assert, "Adam, you said it yourself. It would take a miracle for them to find us. I've gotta go." I leave them the canteen, saying one last thing to Adam, "You'd do anything to get out of makin' that speech, wouldn't ya?"

We see Charles and Garvey riding along in the wagon. They are met by two guys on horseback who are also looking for the missing stagecoach. There are four roads to choose from: two to the north and two behind them. They split up so as to cover all of them. Charles and Garvey double-back to cover the other two.

I am frantically trying to make my way back to the road. I fall and roll down the hill. Wow. I'm tough. I really *did* that!

Poor Mary. She gets beaten by branches, trips on rocks; almost cries, but she keeps going. Climbing now. On hands and knees. Poor *me*!

Charles and Garvey talk about which of the two roads to check first. It doesn't matter either way, as Adam and Mary won't make their train connection now.

Garvey says, "Sure feel sorry for them kids. They were looking forward to this trip."

Charles agrees. "Sure were."

I am still climbing, and boy am I moving along at a good clip. Scary! I try to climb up a cliff and fall backwards; my glasses come flying out of my pocket. I have hit my head and am knocked out cold.

Birds have begun circling the crash site. The camera pans down inside the overturned coach to see Marge praying to God to save her baby.

The reflection off the lenses of my eyeglasses hitting the sun ignites a fire in the dry grass. I wake to the smoke and flames right near me. This fire was so hot, I actually asked to be positioned a bit further away.

Garvey spots smoke on the road to Sanborn. They decide to go that way first.

They hear screaming, "Help me, please! Somebody!"

I am surrounded by flames.

Charles says, "That's Mary!"

That fire almost gets me, but Pa runs in, scoops me up, and gets me outta there.

Back in Winoka it is nighttime at the School for the Blind. Ma, Pa, and I are awaiting news from Dr. Baker. He comes downstairs and tells us that Adam needs time for his fractures to heal. Marge has given birth to a bouncing baby boy.

I say, "It's a *double* miracle."

Pa says, "It's a good thing Mary started that fire. If we hadn't seen that smoke, we'd a never found her."

"I didn't start that fire, Pa."

"Well, then how did it start?" Pa questions.

"I don't know," I answer as I start up the stairs to see Adam.

Caroline and Charles just look at each other, baffled but relieved.

We cut back to the "scene of the crime," where, amidst the charred rock and burned grass, the camera closes in on Mary's glasses.

By the summer of 1979 it had become obvious to our entire cast and crew that Michael Landon was having an affair. For most of our *Little House* "family," the adults in particular, this seemed to be a TV star's midlife crisis. Even taking into account his squeaky-clean, wholesome, family-man image, this was not shocking; he had been married and divorced once before.

But for us, as kids, it was a real blow. Although we knew he could be difficult at times and had his flaws, we never dreamed he was capable of inflicting that kind of pain on his real family. For me personally, I *had* held him up to a higher moral standard. I *believed* all of the hype that he was the greatest husband and father around. He had really let me down. It took me a while to come to terms with the fact that he had fallen off his pedestal and was merely human after all.

I definitely did not like being put in this position. I knew and liked Lynn, his wife. I had too much respect for her to just accept Mike's behavior as "business as usual." But because he was my boss, I tried not to let my personal feelings make too much of an impact on our working relationship.

All bets were off, though, when it came to the "other woman." I just couldn't help it. I *was* sixteen, after all. And Cindy Clerico was *my* stand-in, the person who the cinematographer uses when lighting a scene so as not to unduly tire the actor. She is very small in stature—only about five-foot-one or so. When she was hired as a replacement for my first stand-in, Cindy and I were about the same height, but as I kept growing, she had to increase her heel height so she would be as tall as I was. Stand-ins are required to be as similar to the actor/actress they are standing in for as possible. The same height, coloring, hair color, etc. Even in her platform shoes, she didn't come close to Lynn's height, which meant that Mike ran around in tennis shoes a lot more often. He no longer needed his lifts off-camera.

Cindy and I had been very friendly before the affair became known. She was very athletic and very tan, and she looked great in her teeny Chemin de Fer jeans. We used to commiserate about the best ways to keep our jeans from stretching out. Our pants were so tight, we'd have to lie down and use *pliers* in order to zip them! When I filmed the movie for television, *The Survival of Dana,* I wore those jeans, and I never sat down, ever. I don't know how we ever lived without that fantastic s-t-r-e-t-c-h they have in denim now that makes them bounce right back into shape. Do I sound old?

Anyway, Cindy was always nice, and she did her job. I remember that she had a light-blue Volkswagen Bug when she started. Later, she had a Porsche, and I thought she must have saved her money. I was naïve, I know.

Lynn Landon hired a private detective and found out about the affair. Divorce was imminent. As I worked less on *Little House,* I found that I had yet another stand-in because Cindy had now become a makeup artist. Forgive me for saying this, but I *did* think at the time that it must have sounded better to say you were leaving your wife of nineteen years for a makeup artist than a stand-in.

In my silent show of solidarity with Lynn Landon, I did *not* have my makeup done by Cindy. And she was good, too. I just couldn't bring myself to do it. I was civil to her, but that's about it. We certainly were no longer friends.

It is interesting, albeit sad, to witness a celebrity's fall from grace. I believe that it's human nature to want to see people succeed to great heights. The celebrities involved in these scandals always seem so defensive; they never *said* they were perfect. But *we* think they should be because we *want* them to be; we want them to be role models. In the end, they are just the same as you and me, and I don't know many people who could withstand the kind of scrutiny that celebrities are subject to these days.

On one of my breaks from *Little House*, I went to New York to do publicity for the show. I was there over my seventeenth birthday, and among the gifts I received was a telegram informing me that I had won the Emmy Award for *Which Mother is Mine?* Not a bad gift, I'd say, and I was thrilled.

I became very frustrated playing a "blind pioneer." In the beginning, when Mary first lost her sight and for perhaps one more season, it was a challenge that was both exciting and gratifying. But now, well into the second season of Mary's blindness, I could tell that the writers were having trouble coming up with ideas for Mary and Adam. You know you're in trouble when your character is suffering more tragedies than on a soap opera. This was the problem: It was either feast or famine. Another terrible tragedy or an episode where I was in a scene only to remind the audience that my character is still alive. It was extremely limiting. I couldn't really blame the writers—between the era in which the show was set and my character being blind, there wasn't a lot they could have me do.

I had that seven-year contract. Who would have ever thought I'd be considering an *eighth* year? It was a lot to think about, and I was glad to have the luxury of time in which to make this decision.

As it turned out, it didn't take as long as I'd expected. I read the script for an episode entitled, "Annabelle," and my mind was made up. My character appears in two scenes—one in the blind school and the second at a circus, which has come to Walnut Grove. I speak one line of dialogue in the entire episode: I ask, "What happened?" while at the circus. This was precisely what I did not want to occur. I did not want my character to make "appearances" just for the sake of audience recognition. I would fulfill my seven-year commitment, but I decided to appear only in two episodes during the eighth season.

"May We Make Them Proud," Parts 1 and 2, were written and directed by Mike. These were not my favorites of the shows he had written, but I thought that his acting was particularly good in them. Part 1 opens on a charity picnic to raise funds for the Harriet Oleson Institute for the Advancement of Blind Children and its new addition.

Albert and his friend Clay decide that they're going to practice smoking a pipe because "women like a man who smokes a pipe." While everyone is enjoying themselves outdoors, these two sneak downstairs to the basement of the blind school. They proceed to light up, sharing the pipe and coughing. Hester-Sue interrupts them, and they drop the pipe so she doesn't see. She tells them to get on back outside, now. They skedaddle.

That lit pipe has been dropped into a box containing scraps of fabric and is slowly beginning to smolder. Thin wisps of smoke rise into the air.

The picnic is a huge success, and later Hester-Sue and Alice Garvey, played by Hersha Parady, are finishing the big clean-up. Adam is upstairs tucking the children into their beds and says goodnight. He comes into our room where I am marveling at our beautiful baby and his really strong grip. I will meet Adam and Hester-Sue and Alice downstairs for tea just as soon as I change the baby.

In the basement, the smoldering has now become flames, and a fire has broken out.

As they drink their tea, we see that the fire is now big, and Adam thinks that he smells smoke. Hester-Sue checks the tea kettle and attributes the smell to the fact that all the water had boiled out of it. But Adam notices that the smell is even stronger now. Hester-Sue opens the door to the basement. Flames escape, fire erupts and spreads quickly.

She screams, "Adam! Adam!"

Alice says, "Oh my God! Water! We need buckets!"

But Hester-Sue replies, "It's too late. Get the children!"

Adam bursts through the bedroom door. I am still sitting on the edge of the bed, cooing at the baby in the cradle.

He urges, "Mary, come on. There's a fire. We have to get the kids out."

He pulls me with him.

I must have had some sort of discussion with Mike about this scene because I am *right* in front of that cradle. *Why* don't I grab the baby when Adam tells me about the fire? These are the kinds of arguments you don't win, though, and I must not have, because Mike did not move me to another part of the room where I wouldn't have been so close to that baby.

We hurriedly escort the children out of their rooms and down the hallway toward the staircase. As we pass our bedroom, I hear my baby cry. Alice tells me to go ahead—*she* will get the baby.

Alice enters the bedroom and walks over to the cradle.

She hears a child yelling, "Get me out! Somebody get me out!"

She *leaves the baby* and runs out of the room to the bathroom down the hall.

Again, I have a real problem with this. This just would not happen.

The door is jammed, but she manages to force it open and get the boy out. She leads him down the hallway to the stairs and goes back for my baby.

Alice picks up little Adam Jr,. but by this time, it is too late. The fire is everywhere. She cannot get out of the room. And now the fire is in there, too. She is helpless. She goes to the window and starts to smash the glass, attempting to . . .? She is on the second floor with a tiny baby, surrounded by flames. Even if someone hears her cries for help, there won't be anything they can do.

When Hester-Sue sees James coming down the porch stairs, she quickly runs up to him and realizes that Alice is still inside. She tries to go back up to the second floor, but it is completely engulfed in flames. She makes her way back down the stairs and outside.

Hester-Sue sees Alice and the baby at that second floor window, surrounded by flames. She screams, "Oh my God, the baby!"

Adam and I understand what has happened. Adam fights Hester-Sue to get back into that house. She doesn't let him go in.

It is about sun-up.

The aftermath.

Burning, charred embers.

Everything gone.

Ma tries to be of comfort. She wants to take me home, but I won't go without my baby. Pa finds the child; I ask to hold him. I take Adam Jr. and begin to hum the lullaby from the music box that was his favorite.

Dr. Baker walks through the charred remains of the blind school and into where the basement used to be. He finds a charred pipe and shows it to Charles, who says, "A pipe. A stupid pipe."

Doc Baker says, "Somebody, for some reason, just threw it away."

Charles asks the doctor for some sleeping powders for Mary. "She doesn't even cry. She just sits."

Doc Baker says, "Shock." He knows that she needs time. He'll see that she gets the medicine she needs.

Charles tells the doctor, "We'll notify the parents starting tomorrow. Make arrangements to get them home."

Dr. Baker says, "What chance is there to rebuild?"

Charles replies, "School this size'll take years."

Jonathan Garvey and his son, Andrew (played by Patrick Labyorteaux, Matthew's brother, who grew up to play Lt. Bud Roberts on *JAG*), are mourning, as well. Dr. Baker tries to console them.

Garvey says, "Promise me, Doc. No pine box. Somethin' pretty."

And Doc Baker responds, "I promise."

That night in the Little House, Pa is talking with Laura.

She asks him, "Why, Pa?"

"I don't know why, Half Pint, but," he continues, "I *do* know how. Dr. Baker said he found a pipe down in the basement. That's where the fire started."

Albert has overheard this conversation. He continues listening as Laura says, "A pipe?"

To which Pa responds, "Yeah. Somebody was down there smoking it. For some reason, they just threw it away. I don't think we'll ever know who it was."

Albert walks into the room and says, "I think I'm gonna go to bed now."

He climbs the ladder to the loft. Those words are replaying in his mind. He is horrified.

In our hotel room, I am sleeping fitfully. I wake up and do not remember what has happened. Adam tries to give me a sedative, but I have become so agitated that I knock the glass out of his hands, sending it crashing to the floor.

I tell him, "I want my baby."

He tries to explain what has happened. When he finally comes out with it, I throw a fit and scream and get up, and as I am flailing around, I hit Adam, POW, in the face. As I watch this, I think this was an accident, because it really looks and *sounds* real. I hope I apologized to poor Linwood! I keep on going, tearing up the room. I get to the window, ripping the curtains right off the wall. I smash my fists through the glass panes. Nellie bursts into the room.

Adam barks, "Go get Dr. Baker!"

The next morning at the Little House, Albert begs not to have to go to the funeral. Charles sees how very upset he is and lets him off the hook.

The family, minus Albert, drives up to the hotel to meet with Adam and me. Dr. Baker is waiting for them out front. They inquire as to how I am feeling this morning.

"I'd like to talk to you about that before you go on up."

When they come inside, he tells them, "Mary's had a breakdown of sorts."

"She doesn't believe her baby's dead. And she won't go to the funeral."

Charles says, "She has to."

Dr. Baker goes on to explain, "She believes her child is alive, and we're all lying to her."

Caroline says, "I'll go to her."

And lastly, the doctor says, "She doesn't respond to anything."

Caroline walks into our room and tries to cajole me out of bed. All I do is pull the covers back up and start humming.

But at least I'm in tune!

The funeral takes place, and the last of the blind children are being sent back to their respective homes. Adam goes to see Caroline and the family. The poor guy really needs to talk.

"It's been two weeks now, and there's just no change. She hasn't spoken. She just keeps humming that lullaby. I can't stand seeing her like this anymore."

Adam is drained. He continues, telling Caroline that he has telephoned his father in New York, and he would like to take Mary there to see doctors who specialize in just this type of thing. Adam will go himself first. He needs a break. A few days to himself "to try and get my strength back," he says.

Albert doesn't know what to do with all of this guilt that he feels.

Charles and Jonathan make their way home from Mankato after delivering a shipment there. They stop; take a break. Charles tells Jonathan that he'd like him to attend church with the family, stating, "It helps, believe me."

Jonathan blames God for taking his Alice, for not stopping that fire. All those miracles in the Bible—why didn't He perform one the other night?

Caroline and Charles discuss the prospect of Adam and me going back East. They don't want me to go, but of course they want to do whatever is best for me. Psychiatry is a new idea for them—but worth a try.

Albert seems close to tears all the time, and Jonathan Garvey is drinking too much; in front of his son—it doesn't matter. Andy tries to help his dad, but Garvey is always angry.

He yells, "Just go on to school!"

What a mess we all are.

Albert comes to look after me, relieving Ma of this duty, as I cannot be left alone. I just sit in bed. He brings a book that he knows I like and begins to read aloud. I start that humming again. This is the end of Part 1. *Not* the most exciting cliffhanger, I'd say.

Part 2 begins with Albert working furiously on his chores in the barn. Pa asks him to go with him on a trip to Tracy, but the boy adamantly says no, he does *not* want to go. He only wants to be with Mary. He can't tell Pa why he is so upset all the time. He just says he doesn't know.

Pa is now worried about the mental health of *two* of his children. He tries to be understanding and patient with Albert, but he *does* insist that the boy accompany him on this day trip. He would like the company, he says.

In Tracy the following day, Pa wants to buy Albert a brand-new boy's rifle, but Albert sees a music box that plays the lullaby I keep humming. He asks Pa if he could buy that instead as a gift for Mary. What's the guy gonna say? No?

When the two arrive back at the Little House, Caroline tells Charles that Andrew Garvey is inside and Charles should really talk to the boy. Can't this guy ever get a break?

Andy tells Charles that his pa is drinking more and getting meaner. The poor kid doesn't know whether to stay or go. He's afraid. Charles tells him that he will go there and talk with his pa.

Albert comes to look after me and proudly gives me his gift.

"Mary, please open it. I know you'll like it."

I am ignoring him; won't open the gift.

He says, "*I'll* open it. I know you'll like it. It'll make ya laugh; make you smile again. Everything'll be the way it was." He has unwrapped the beautiful music box. He opens the lid, saying, "You listen, now. I know it's your favorite. Do you like it? Please say you like it, Mary, please."

I listen. That's it. I crack. I start screaming, "My baby!" Over and over. I am scaring the poor kid out of his mind. As if he didn't feel bad enough already. Albert backs out of the room, screaming himself, now: "I didn't mean it! I didn't mean it! It was an accident. Oh, I didn't mean it!"

Matthew sure was a good child actor. Whew!

Meanwhile, Charles goes to see Jonathan, who is drinking, of course, and looking at old photo albums. He says, "Dear God. Am I supposed to forget her?"

Charles answers, "Oh, no. Never forget her. Time doesn't make you forget. Not somebody you loved. You're gonna remember Alice, and I'm gonna remember my grandson. But we're gonna live on. And we gotta try to live in a way that will make them proud. We gotta try."

He goes on to tell him that his son needs him. When he hurts Andy, he's hurting Alice—and himself.

Laura runs up to the Garvey home to tell Pa the news. Mary got "real upset; Doc Baker's with her. Pa, she talked. She *talked*."

It seems that all Pa does is put out one fire after the other. OOOH. That was bad. No pun intended.

We cut to the hotel room where I am starting to awaken. I admit now that "My baby's dead." I tell them that I know there was a fire.

I say, "It was the music. I heard the music."

Ma says, "The music box that Albert gave you?"

"Albert. Where is he?" I ask.

Ma explains that I frightened him and he probably went home.

Dr. Baker says, "You were pretty violent when I got here, young lady."

I tell them, "He kept saying something to me like, 'It was an accident; I didn't mean it.' He kept saying it."

Hester-Sue says, "I didn't say anything. I didn't think of it, really. But I went down to the basement that day and Albert *was* there with Clay Mays. I shooed 'em out, but . . ."

Things are beginning to make sense now. Charles leaves to find Albert. He is not at home, so Charles asks Garvey to come with him to help look for Albert. The two men go to Clay's home, waking the boy up to ask him what really happened that day. Clay was played by Billy Calvert, who also had a small role in another project with me, *An Innocent Love.* The boy hesitantly tells them that he "snitched Mr. Potts's pipe, and we was smokin.'"

So now they know.

Charles can only say, "Dear God."

Charles, Jonathan, and Caroline sit around the table trying to figure out where Albert could have gone. Charles thinks that he'd go to Judge Adams's office in Redwood City, knowing he'd be able to get the address of his *real* father there. Even though his biological father doesn't care much about Albert, Charles thinks that this is the only place he has to go. So, Charles and Garvey leave to look for the boy there.

Charles is right, as we see that the boy has just arrived at the judge's office. The secretary informs Albert that the judge is not in as yet, but he can wait in his office. Albert knows exactly where the office is; this is where his adoption with the Ingalls's took place. He enters the office, goes over to the file cabinet, and finds his own adoption file. Albert finds what he is looking for and is on his way.

By the time Charles and Garvey arrive at Judge Adams's office, the judge himself is coming in to work. The judge is inclined to think that kids who run away usually go back to their old stomping grounds. He asks them if they are sure the boy didn't go back to Winoka. They can't believe he'd go that far but decide that they'll go partway and ask around, then check back with the judge.

There is finally a lull in Judge Adams's day, so his secretary takes this opportunity to talk to him about the little boy who waited in his office early that morning. She presumed that the judge had seen Albert; obviously she was wrong. The judge asks her to send for his driver right away.

We see that Albert has hitched a ride out to his father's place, where he looks all around and calls out, "Mr. Quinn?" He walks around the property but sees no one. Finally, he spots what seems to be a cross out in the yard. He goes over to it. It is a grave. His biological father is dead.

Judge Adams has sent a note to Charles via messenger. The boy *has* gone to look for his father after all. Garvey and Charles go after him.

Albert has been sleeping in the barn. He awakens, sees their wagon, and runs. And runs. And runs.

Caught! By Merlin Olsen's Jonathan Garvey. Not gonna get out of *his* grip.

"It was all my fault," Albert cries to Jonathan.

"You're blamin' yourself for what happened. Just like my blamin' God for what happened. And we're *both* wrong. And all this runnin' is just hurtin' them that loves you the most. And addin' more pain to what they've already got. Do you understand that, boy?"

"I can't go back."

And Jonathan says, basically what Charles told *him*. "You gotta hold the memory of the ones you love and try and make them proud."

Charles has caught up to them. He immediately tells Albert that he loves him. The boy runs to him; they hug.

After Sunday's church service (conveniently held at the site of the tragedy), Adam delivers a short speech. He says that while he was back East, his father asked to be allowed to finance the rebuilding of the Blind School. He made one request—that he be allowed to name the new school.

A plaque is unveiled. It reads:

THE ALICE GARVEY
ADAM KENDALL JR.
SCHOOL FOR THE BLIND

Adam says, "And may we make them proud."

Well, there were many good performances in this two-parter, and this was a nice ending. Can't say much more than that.

On my hiatus, I shot my third *Love Boat* and an episode of Father Elwood Kaiser's *Insight* program, where I think I was the "bad girl" and even smoked! I also filmed an episode of *Fantasy Island*. I don't remember what it was about, but I *do* remember working with the great character actor Michael Constantine. And Ricardo Montalban . . . what can I say? Smooth as silk and completely charming and nice. What a pleasure it was to work with him.

And, before I knew it, I was back to work on Season Seven of *Little House.*

SEASON SEVEN
May 1980–January 1981

CHAPTER EIGHTEEN

"Blind Justice" and
Happy Birthday to Me

In the spring of 1980, I got some of the best news I'd ever gotten. I was set to star in my first feature film, *Happy Birthday To Me,* for Columbia Pictures and directed by J. Lee Thompson of *Guns of Navarone* fame. This was not the first time I'd been offered the lead in a feature film, however. I was originally asked to play the role Brooke Shields made famous in *The Blue Lagoon* a couple of years earlier. I was uncomfortable with the nudity, though, not to mention the fact that I had a morals clause in my NBC contract. So I politely turned it down.

This time it wasn't as difficult to solve the scheduling conflict with *Little House* because I simply wasn't in as many episodes that season. I was also just lucky that the majority of those shows were already set to be filmed *after* I would have finished shooting the movie.

So, from June through August, I was in Montreal working hard, filming this movie, and loving every minute of it. As a matter of fact, the hotel where I stayed is just a ways down the street from where I live now.

When I first arrived, I had the usual wardrobe fittings that are standard before beginning any production. I also had a makeup test, which I hadn't had before, to determine my look with the lighting that would be used in the film with the cinematographer, gaffer, and Lee, the director. This test was conducted on the set of my character Virginia Wainwright's bedroom. I remember that it was very pretty and very realistic as a teenage girl's room. But, hey, after spending so many years in an 1870s loft, *anything* would have looked good to me.

There was a lot of film production going on in Montreal at that time, and the town was bustling with all of the activity. I remember meeting Howie Mandel, who was in town shooting a comedy at the time. He was very nice—cute and funny—and his wife Terry was with him as she is today. There's a working Hollywood marriage for ya.

I worked with many talented young Canadian actors and actresses, a few who have gone on to have long careers in film and television. Matt Craven works all the time, and Lawrence Dane (who played my father) was a bad guy in one of my *Equalizer* episodes.

About halfway through the production, Lee told me that the studio thought I was so convincing as the good girl, Ginny, they didn't want to sacrifice the audience's sympathy for me by turning me bad, as originally intended. Aw, shoot, I thought. I *loved* playing the bad girl, but there wasn't much I could do about this turn of events.

As a direct result of this major script change, I now had to be fitted for special effects makeup. I'm not sure "fitted" is the right word, but what I mean is having a plaster cast made of my entire head so that a latex mask could be fashioned from it. The new "bad girl" would supposedly be wearing this mask when she commits all kinds (and I do mean *all* kinds) of gruesome murders.

It was really me, of course, playing both roles. The "bad girl" is only revealed at the end when removing that infamous mask.

A word of caution: When filming in cemeteries in the dead of night (pun intended), be sure to wear mosquito repellent. I counted sixty-seven bites on my legs from my knees down to my ankles. Unbelievably itchy—I was still scratching on the plane ride home.

You would think I'd be immune to the effects of scary movies after my experiences shooting *Happy Birthday* and *Midnight Offerings*, but no. I am a complete wuss, a real scaredy-cat. I am the first to scream; that person who scares the *rest* of the audience!

Happy Birthday To Me was released in May of 1981, and I saw it in the theater with all of my friends. We took up an entire row!

The late J. Lee Thompson was a master at building suspense. He made a good and scary movie of which we were all very proud and happy—no one happier than Frank Price, the president of Columbia, as our film did well at the box office.

I returned to *Little House* for "To See The Light" Parts 1 and 2, written and directed by Mike Landon.

The camera follows as a wagon hauling explosives and marked DANGER rides into town and parks. These crates of explosives are carefully unloaded and placed in the storage area beside Garvey's office in Sleepy Eye, where the School for the Blind has relocated. Hester-Sue and Adam go to Jonathan Garvey's office looking for him and the school's new Braille readers. Garvey seems to be out, so they take it upon themselves to look for the crates of books.

Hester-Sue quickly finds them, but she and Adam soon discover they are just too heavy to carry. They decide to open them there and make a few trips back and forth. Adam tells Hester-Sue that there should be a crowbar in the office for them to use to open the crates. She is having difficulty finding one. Adam is sure Garvey keeps them there and instinctively takes a step forward as he talks. He trips over something, and he goes careening into the very volatile crates of blasting oil. We cut to the exterior of the building just as a big explosion comes from inside.

At the hospital, I am waiting with Hester-Sue for news about Adam. Finally, a Dr. Raymond comes to speak with us. He tells me that the operation went as planned and that Adam has an excellent chance for recovery. He did lose a lot of blood, and he has suffered a bad concussion. They will know more in a few days. The doctor gives me the okay to go in and sit with him.

In the hospital room, I sit in a chair next to Adam's bed. I go on and on and on, willing him to live: "You're my life. I couldn't live without you. I need you."

Is it me, or is this just a tad over the top? It *is* probably me. I was so worn out with all of these tragedies. It *still* gets to me now—just watching it.

Meanwhile, at Nellie's restaurant, Nellie is pregnant and is chastised by her husband, Percival, when he finds her sneaking ice cream. He tells her, "Maybe your father doesn't care that your mother's fat, but I don't want you following in her footsteps."

Mrs. Oleson gets involved and says, "I'm not fat. I'm large-boned."

Percival quips, "That would be rather difficult to determine, since your bones are buried so deep beneath the surface."

So there.

Caroline receives a phone call about Adam's accident and tells Hester-Sue that she and Charles will be on their way first thing the next morning.

Harriet greets Nels as he drives up in the buggy.

"Nels?"

"Yes, dear?"

"Can I ask you a question?"

"Yes, dear."

"Do you think I'm fat?"

"Yes, dear."

Back and forth they go. Finally Nels tells Harriet she's "pleasingly plump."

Harriet wails, "I don't want to be pleasingly plump!"

The next day, Ma and Pa have arrived to support me in my vigil for Adam. The camera sees Adam in his hospital bed. He wakes up, looks around. He sits up. He calls for me.

"Mary."

"Mary."

"Mary!"

He walks outside his room into the hallway. The nurses try to stop him but cannot. Adam *sees* Jonathan and plants a big kiss on him as he rants, "I can see. I can see!"

Cut to the exterior of the town and Jonathan Garvey at a full-out sprint down the middle of the street. He gets to the blind school and says excitedly, "Mary. He can see. Adam can see!"

Ma, Pa, and I are at the hospital, talking with the doctor.

Pa says, "It's a miracle."

The doctor says, "There is a medical explanation. Adam lost his sight from a concussion. His sight was restored the same way."

Pa confirms, "To me, that's a miracle."

I believe this is reminiscent of Little Joe's blindness on *Bonanza*.

It's hard for me to comprehend that my husband will be able to *see* me.

I enter the room. I sit next to the bed; let him know I'm there.

He says, "Oh, my beautiful Mary."

I am relieved that he seems to like what he sees.

"You're so beautiful, more beautiful than I'd ever imagined."

Sweet talker.

As I watch this, I chuckle a bit, looking at my horrible hairdo. In the fall, after filming *Happy Birthday*, I decided to "take the plunge" and cut my hair. This was a risky thing to do because I didn't ask permission, and I knew the hairdressing department would *not* be happy. But, I figured, I didn't have that many episodes left to shoot. Other than being mad at me, there wouldn't be much else they could do.

As a teenage girl, I'd always had hair issues. We always want what we don't have. You've already heard about my "Farrah wings." Later, when I prepared to shoot *The Survival of Dana*, I thought that it would be great to get a perm, so as to have two different looks for the movie. The "nice girl," with softer, blown-out hair, and the "wild girl," with curly, cooler hair. This was an interesting idea but a bit harder to achieve than I had expected.

Those were the days when we didn't have flat irons, to iron out curls and frizz. We had only round brushes and blow-dryers, and it was an arduous process trying to make those pretty waves and curls straight again. Later, I found that using electric rollers worked really well. They completely took out the frizz, and I had long, big curls. I'd graduated from Farrah Fawcett to Jaclyn Smith!

Anyway, this time I cut my hair short. It was above my shoulders, and I had graduated layers around my face. I loved it. I finally got up the courage to call our hairdresser, Larry Germain, to tell him the news.

He said something like, "Oh, you did, did you?"

And I could almost hear the smile on his face. He measured me for a long wig (for those bed scenes) and also for a piece that would be my "knot," or bun, on the back of my head. Whew! What a relief to have that over with.

I should have known I'd gotten off too easy. My punishment was that once they'd styled my short pieces, pinning and pinning and tucking them in, I looked like I had a mushroom on my head. Uggh. Awful. Just awful. And don't even ask what I looked like when they took me apart at the end of the day. Gone were the days of going out right after work. I was a mess with all these strange dents and bends in my new haircut. I had to wash it and start all over just to be able to go to the grocery store or the dry cleaners. I could feel a few pangs of regret beginning to creep my way.

Getting back to the story, Nellie is amazed at how well her mother is doing on her diet. Mrs. O. says, "Willpower, darling. Once your mother makes up her mind to stick to something, she sticks to it."

Wearing her waitress hat, Mrs. Oleson places an order for two plates of ham and eggs, which Nellie cooks. Mrs. O. delivers one plate to a table and sneaks off with the other into the small switchboard office just off the dining room. She is just about to dig in ravenously when she is interrupted by Nellie. She quickly hides the plate. Nellie goes on about the fact that *she* is always hungry; she even thinks she smells ham and eggs right now. Mrs. O. tells Nellie to go and rest for a while. She just wants to eat her breakfast already! Her daughter leaves finally, and Mrs. Oleson prepares to eat the delicious . . . but that darned telephone rings. Mrs. O. barks into it, "Walnut Grove!!" then, hearing the news from Caroline, is off like a shot. Running up the street to tell Laura Adam's wonderful news. The plate of ham and eggs falls off the back of her skirt; the evidence is all over her.

Back at the blind school, my husband wants to take me out for a drive. As we ride along, Adam remarks on all of the colors—more vivid than he remembers. And my eyes: "I've never seen eyes as blue as yours."

He says, "Mary, do you realize what my seeing is gonna mean to us? All the places we can go now; we couldn't before? We won't have to rely on anybody. Just you and me. There's nothing we can't do."

Adam is so excited that he decides to run around the country-side. He runs and runs. He pronounces the world "wonderful."

That night, I sit talking with Ma and Pa. Ma asks, "Mary, is something wrong?"

"It's just gonna take a little getting used to. Adam's sight, I mean. It's like meeting someone again for the first time. He can see me and I can't see him. It's a very strange feeling."

Ma wisely says, "For both of you. Remember, Adam's gonna have a lot of adjusting to do, too."

Adam is back teaching. As a student answers one of his questions, Adam is drawn to the window. He is easily distracted by the world out there. He asks the children to spend the next half-hour reading quietly. He goes for a walk. He sees the Courthouse and the sign that reads COURT IN SESSION. He enters and takes a seat in the courtroom.

The actor portraying the defense attorney is almost screaming every one of his lines.

Definitely not *Law and Order*.

Adam is fascinated by these proceedings and continues to watch.

The case concludes with a victory for the defense attorney, and Adam hurries out to congratulate him. He tells Adam that his client was guilty; rightly assuming that Adam would be surprised by that fact. Adam tells the lawyer that he intended to study the law years ago, and the attorney invites him to a lawn party at his home on Saturday.

Adam finally arrives back at the blind school some four hours later. I am beginning to prepare dinner.

"Where have you been?" I ask, concerned.

Adam explains about his afternoon in court and talking with the lawyer afterwards. He tells me that Mr. Davis even invited us to his home on Saturday, forgetting about an outing we had planned with the children.

Hester-Sue quickly says she can manage it on her own, and Adam happily pleads, "You say yes, and I'll cook the whole dinner."

As he starts cooking, I am still unsure of all of this.

We arrive at the lawn party. Adam plays croquet with the champion, Mrs. Davis. But not for long, as Adam beats her.

I am sitting alone.

Now, it's badminton. Adam is having the time of his life.

Late that night, I am in bed as Adam recounts his fun day. He excitedly goes on and on about Mr. Davis and the party.

"Ya ever see so much food in your life? Lobster all the way from New York. Musta' cost a fortune, just to ship it out here."

Adam talks about Mr. Davis trying a case against the railroad.

"What a feeling that must be—going up against the railroad and winning. You know, just one time in my life I'd like to know what that feels like. Just once."

I manage to get a word in to ask what he thinks about us taking the children out to the lake next Saturday, to catch fish and have a cookout.

Adam answers, "It's just that Mr. Davis invited us again, for next Saturday. There are gonna be some other attorneys there. Thought it might be interesting."

"I really don't think we should miss two Saturdays in a row."

I am not happy.

"I suppose not," Adam sighs.

Then I cave, and in the end, we compromise. Adam will go to the lawn party. I'll go fishing with the kids and Hester-Sue. He will "be there in time to cook the fish. Don't worry about that."

It is Saturday, late afternoon. Hester-Sue is taking pieces of fish off the fire and serving seconds to anyone who has room left. I am standing on a little bridge over the water. Hester-Sue sees me and approaches.

"I'm losing him, Hester Sue."

"What on earth are you talking about?" she asks.

"I'm losing Adam to his new friends—his *sighted* friends."

She tries to defend him. "That's not true. He *wanted* you to go with him."

"Not really. When he's with his sighted friends, I don't even exist. I'm afraid, Hester Sue. Afraid of losing my husband to a world I can't see."

I *do* have a point.

In the kitchen that night, Adam dares to, I mean Adam walks in and wants to talk.

Oh, really.

He starts, "I used to love teaching. I found it challenging and exciting and I really thought that's what I wanted to do for the rest of my life. But it just isn't." He goes on to say he wants to be a lawyer. "I *have* to be a lawyer. Mr. Davis is arranging for me to go to Minneapolis to take the law exam, and if I get a good enough grade, I've got a chance at a scholarship."

This is an awful lot for me to take in.

"Mary, I want this more than I've wanted anything in my whole life. And I can do it. I just *know* I can do it."

To say that I am surprised would be an understatement.

Adam goes for the big finish. "I've got this feeling, it's like God came down and gave me back my sight and then said, okay, let's see what you can do with it."

And he's off to start studying.

Part 1 ends with the concerned look on my face. Part 2 begins as Adam studies. And studies. He reads while dishing up food for the children as they wait in line. I tell Adam that most of the children will be going home for the summer break.

"I thought I'd go home for a few weeks—visit the family," I say.

Adam and I decide that he'll take the stage directly from Minneapolis as soon as he completes his exam so that we'll be able to spend a little time together.

Adam is consumed by his need to become a lawyer. He thinks that will solve any problem we could ever have.

At Nellie's restaurant, Mrs. Oleson needs Nellie to help lace up her corset so she can have a chance of fitting into the new dress that she ordered in a smaller size. Since Nellie can't leave her cooking, they begin this process in the pantry, but as food needs to be tended to, they must move around the kitchen—Mrs. O. in slip and corset.

Nellie turns her full attention to the corset. She pulls and she tugs, but she can't get it as tight as her mother would like. She needs more leverage. She puts one foot on her mother's back; that's better. She pulls and pulls and tugs some more. Almost there. Just about tight enough, when . . . SNAP! The laces break and Mrs. O. goes flying out of the kitchen and into the dining room, smacking head-first right into a plate of food. Laughter erupts. She grabs the tablecloth to cover herself and runs out of the restaurant, crossing just in front of the stagecoach, which is arriving in town with me aboard. Jack Lilley is the driver this time.

Ma comes out to greet me and is trying to be helpful settling me in at the hotel.

I bite her head off, saying, "There are some things blind people can do!" Then I apologize, telling her that "I don't know what's the matter with me."

Ma says not to worry about Adam passing the exam: "I'm sure he'll do very well."

But I say, "I don't want him to do well."

"What?" Ma can't believe what she's hearing.

"I don't want him to go to law school. I want him to stay home with me, with the children. We need him."

Ma patiently replies, "Mary, this is a once-in-a-lifetime chance for Adam. I know it'll be difficult being apart for awhile, but . . . you have your whole lives to be together."

But I go on. "I'm afraid that now that he can see, he'll think I'm a burden to him. He'll be meeting new people—new women . . ."

Ma jumps on that, saying, "The only one who could destroy that love is you."

Does that mean Mary can't feel sorry for herself anymore?

Ma continues, "You're his wife. You stand by him, help him. Blind or sighted, he needs your love and your strength. Land sakes, girl! Thought ya had more guts than that."

Pep talk concluded; she convinces me to call Adam.

The next day we see Adam as he arrives in Minneapolis to take the law exam. He has managed to survive his first six hours of testing and exits the building, tiredly sinking onto the first bench he sees.

He makes a friend, Alan Barton, played by Donald Petrie who is now a popular film director, directing such hits as *Mystic Pizza* and *Miss Congeniality*. Alan invites Adam to join him for dinner and gives him a ride back to the train that evening. Poor Adam gets mugged as he waits for the train. He is knocked out and unconscious, once again.

He wakes up and asks, "Where am I?" The nurse tells him that he's in the hospital.

Adam asks, "What time is it?"

He is told that it is 8:30 a.m.—he has to be at the exam by 9:00 a.m. He's outta there.

The nurse says, "Get back in that bed." She runs to get the doctor.

Adam leaves the hospital and runs and runs in the pouring rain. He finally gets there—late, but he squeaks in by the skin of his teeth.

At the end of that exam day, his new friend offers his home for Adam to stay in, since all of his money was stolen. Adam gratefully accepts, and they grab a cab, horse-drawn, of course.

At the opulent home of Alan's father, a judge, he offers Adam soup, but Adam just wants to sleep. Day turns to night; he is still asleep. His friend comes to check on Adam and calls for the doctor. Adam is sick. The next time that Adam awakens, it is 8:00 a.m.—three days later. He was very sick. He missed the last two days of the exam.

The good news: Alan passed. This was his fourth time! He will telephone Mary to let her know about Adam.

Back in Walnut Grove, Mrs. O. is ravenous—again. She goes scrounging around in the restaurant's pantry. She sees something that she loves. No, too fattening. Keeps looking. Finds . . . that's it, popcorn!

"Yes. It's light. It's not fattening. It's filling."

Katherine McGregor was very funny in this episode. She used just the right amount of humor, not over the top. She pours some oil into a heavy pot and begins pouring in corn kernels when Nels barges in, scaring Harriet, who dumps the remaining kernels, jar and all, into the pot, covering it quickly with the lid. He has spoiled her party. He even accuses her of sneaking out to come over to Nellie's to eat. Harriet denies everything, of course, and lets Nels drag her away from the kitchen and over to the switchboard.

I am in my room, talking with Ma, lamenting the fact that Adam hasn't called, as he said he would.

Just then, Mrs. Oleson flies in with Minneapolis on the line. I smile.

I get the news about Adam. Ma says she is sure Pa will be able to take me to Minneapolis.

Nels doesn't like being a watchdog. But he is trying to help Harriet lose some weight before her thin and perfect cousin Miriam comes for a visit. He knows that Harriet is embarrassed about her appearance and would really like to look better for her.

Harriet promises not to eat.

Nels says, "All right. I trust you, then. I'm sorry I didn't believe you."

Clang!

Bang!

Harriet has been found out. Popcorn pops out of the pot and scatters everywhere.

Pa and I are on the train. I tell him that I hope Adam can be happy being a teacher again.

We arrive at Alan's home, and I talk to Adam. He is heartbroken. He wanted this so badly. He's afraid he's too old to try again next year, hope again for that scholarship, and *still* have to attend law school.

I talk with Pa. I feel guilty because I really didn't want Adam to pass the exam.

"When I talked to him today, I realized how much it meant to him."

Pa reiterates the rules regarding the law exam, waiting a year to take it again, etc.

"I feel like I've betrayed him in my thoughts. I have to make up for that."

Pa agrees to take me to speak to the professor.

I plead Adam's case—but to no avail. The professor just won't alter this "bad rule" that I tell him "has no compassion or concern for the individual." I continue, telling him that "you may think it's necessary, but I happen to think it's cruel."

As Pa and I leave, "Mrs. Kendall? *You* should've been a lawyer. Have your husband here at 9:00 a.m. on Wednesday."

"Thank you, sir."

Made swift work of that.

It is Wednesday afternoon. Pa and I wait outside for Adam. Finally, he comes out, telling us he waited for the professor to grade his exam.

Unfortunately, he did not make the top three percent needed to get that scholarship. I am disappointed for him, but I quickly say things like, you'll try again next year . . .

Adam interrupts me, saying that he made the top *one* percent!

"Oh, Adam Kendall. I'm gonna kill you!" as I give him a big hug.

In Walnut Grove, the Ingalls clan is preparing a celebration for Adam. The stage arrives early. We get off and go inside the restaurant.

Nels literally must drag Harriet to meet the stage that carries her thin and perfect cousin, Miriam, but when they spot Miriam, Harriet breaks into a wide grin. Thin and perfect cousin Miriam is not so thin after all. She's pleasingly plump, as Nels would say.

And now Harriet has a friend to feast with!

In the fall of 1980, I starred in a Movie of the Week for ABC entitled *Midnight Offerings*, written by Juanita Bartlett and executive-produced by Stephen J. Cannell, both of *The Rockford Files*, which I loved, by the way. I played an evil, contemporary witch. My manager, the late Jay Bernstein, worked out a great deal for me. I starred in the movie but only had to work ten days. Jay was legendary in Hollywood. He began as a press agent, working with Michael Landon, among others. In the 70s, Jay became known as the "Starmaker," and there was even a TV movie made about him. He was instrumental in launching the careers of Farrah Fawcett and Suzanne Somers, and then there was me. People questioned his necessity in my already flourishing career, but he was a smooth talker and convinced me that I needed him. He thought of me as a "young Rita Hayworth." He got me. I was hooked. Jay was very eccentric. He always wore a hunting jacket and carried a walking stick; he must have had hundreds of them. He was famously single until one day, years later, when my husband and I received an invitation to Jay's "underwater wedding." It was unfortunate that we couldn't make it; I bet it was spectacular.

The role in *Midnight Offerings* was fun—it was always a nice change to play a "bad" character. This time I stayed bad, through and through. I wore ritualistic "witch" makeup and wardrobe in some scenes and had to learn the chants and incantations phonetically because they were so hard to pronounce.

The tricky part of this TV movie deal was that I was scheduled to shoot a *Little House* episode on location in Sonora, so complicated logistics had to be worked out.

One day in the middle of the ABC shoot, I was wrapped at lunchtime, so that I could fly up to Sonora to work on an episode called "Blind Justice," where Adam practices law for the first time. As I was being driven from the Mar Vista set to the Santa Monica airport, I removed the "witch" makeup (it *was* creepy) and noticed my *very* long, red fingernails. Hmmm. I *really* hoped the camera wouldn't see my hands on *Little House* because there wouldn't be time to paint the nails again before going back to work on the "witch" movie!

I hopped on a helicopter that took me to the Van Nuys airport where I was met by Mike with Cindy, and we all climbed aboard the Lear Jet that flew us to Sonora, California. During our flight, Mike passed me a Diet Coke and asked the pilot to roll the plane. As we started to roll to one side, I said, "What about my drink? It's going to spill all over the place!"

Mike said, "Wait and see." So we rolled and our drinks stayed right where they were in their glasses. Cool! A very neat feeling, too. Of course the pilot told me not to mention this to anyone, and *mostly* I kept quiet.

After we landed and were driven to the motel, Mike asked if I would like to join them and our producer, Kent McCray, for dinner.

It felt great to be included and also to be an adult and not need a chaperone.

This was the motel where we always stayed each time we shot on location in Sonora. It sat right smack on the two-lane highway and had a swimming pool with a slide adjacent to the parking lot. Cars would be parked right up to the three sides of the building. There were steep concrete stairs on each end with one more level of little rooms. Each room had a sliding glass door that faced the street, two beds on one side of the room and a dresser and desk permanently attached to the wall on the other. The bathroom was directly opposite the sliding glass door. Get the picture? Let's just say it was clean, cozy, and definitely not the Hilton!

We had a nice Italian dinner. Mike could not help but notice the bright red nail polish I was wearing.

He said, "Hey, Missy! You *will* lose the nail polish! Yes?"

I said, "Absolutely!"

Everyone had quite a bit to drink (not me, I was just 18) and headed back to the motel. Kent escorted me to my room but unfortunately didn't want to say goodnight and end it there. He was a big guy—tall and about 325 pounds. I really had a hard time getting him out of the way of my glass door so I could slide it closed. Eventually I was able to politely say goodnight and *lock* my door! Good thing, 'cause I had an early call the next day. I knew he probably wouldn't remember any of this, and of course I never brought it up. I had to face the fact that now that I was legally an adult, these kinds of things might happen occasionally. I didn't take any of it seriously, and I always continued to have a good relationship with Kent.

EXT. COURTHOUSE — DAY

Mary and Adam EXIT down the steps. They move past the camera.

CONTINUED:

                    MAURY DEXTER
                  (calling)
          And . . . Cut!

Missy walks past her chair with MELISSA SUE ANDER-
SON stenciled on it.

EXT. BIG BLUE TRUCK — DAY

Missy climbs up the steps in her period dress.

INT. BIG BLUE TRUCK — DAY

Missy walks straight to the cooler, flips up the
top, peels off one of the gloves, dives into the
ice, and comes up with a TAB. She has not even
noticed there are other people in the truck that
was nicknamed "The Blue Max." She opens the TAB,
lifts it to her lips, turns and stops dead.

REVERSE ANGLE

Mike Landon and Jack Lilley, Horse Wrangler/Some-
time Actor, are standing in the back, smoking a
joint. Both of them look a little nonplussed.

ON MISSY

Shock doesn't begin to describe her reaction. She
wants to disappear. She also wants her red nails
to disappear! She quickly puts that glove back on.

                    MISSY
                  (stammering)
          I, uh . . . came to, uh . . . get a
          TAB and . . . gonna go . . . now . . .

```
CONTINUED:

She leaps to the steps.


EXT. TRUCK — DAY

Missy climbs down the steps on her way to her
chair.

Some of the CREW are standing outside the Court-
house waiting between set-ups. Missy drops into
her chair and takes a swig of TAB.
```

It's kind of a shame that we have to grow up and find out that these people we've always looked up to are just as capable of doing dumb things as the rest of us. I'll never forget that moment or the look on Mike's face. Wow!

"Blind Justice" was written by Carole and Michael Raschella and directed by Maury Dexter, who usually functioned as our first assistant director but moved up to director for this episode.

It's strange for me to watch these later shows, as it's almost like seeing them for the first time. I remember very little—maybe because I was so busy on other projects.

We watch as the stage arrives in Sleepy Eye, and Adam slowly gets out—looking around. Jack Lilley is the driver again and welcomes Adam back home.

Dub Taylor joined our show at the end of Season Six, portraying Houston Lamb, caretaker at the blind school. Houston meets Adam at the stage. He tells Adam that something came up and Mary couldn't make it.

The two come in the front door of the blind school, and we all come out to surprise him. Pa gives him our gift of a sign which reads: ADAM KENDALL, ATTORNEY AT LAW.

After a celebratory feast, Adam and I go to our room, and I ask, "What happens next?"

"Well, Mr. Davis did promise that junior partnership in his firm. First thing in the morning, I guess I go to work."

Adam is off bright and early to meet Mr. Davis, who says, "I can't spare you too much time. I have a lunch meeting with a circuit court judge."

They talk. Mr. Davis condescendingly says that law school must have been especially difficult for someone who had been blind for so long.

Adam lets him know that he graduated in the top one percent of his class.

"Look, I hate to cut this short, but as I told you, I do have this meeting."

Adam explains that he doesn't want to take up his time. "I just wanted to know when I should start."

Mr. Davis hems and haws.

Adam continues, "You do remember saying that if I passed the Bar, there'd be a job waiting for me."

Mr. Davis talks about the fact that he hired someone six weeks ago. Adam can't believe that he would do this: "Mr. Davis, you gave me your word. We had an agreement. I've been counting on this job. We shook *hands* on it."

"Well, I'm sorry."

They move to the door. As they walk through, a woman is waiting just outside the door.

She says, "Ready for lunch, Arthur?"

Adam doesn't miss a beat, saying with sarcasm, "Morning, Your Honor."

Now Adam must pound the pavement looking for work. It is not going well. That night at dinner, we are discussing it. Adam thinks he has come up with a good idea: "I think I should go where I'm needed."

Hester-Sue asks, "Adam, what are you saying?"

Adam replies, "Walnut Grove doesn't have a lawyer."

Leave Sleepy Eye?

Houston says, "With you and Mary gone, what's gonna happen to the school?"

Hester-Sue says, "I was running the school when these two were still listenin' to bedtime stories."

But, I insist, "Hester-Sue, we just can't leave you here."

"Listen, Mary. That sheepskin of his is not wallpaper. And he should use it. Now, if he thinks goin' to Walnut Grove is the thing to do, then you should do it."

Adam would like me to be his secretary.

Not if he knew how badly I type.

"What do you think?' he asks.

"I don't know . . ."

"Your family will be real happy," Hester-Sue says.

"Well?" Adam asks again.

"All right. We'll go."

Later, I talk with Houston. I tell him how I'll miss this school. He doesn't want us to go: "You know, Mary, you've been somethin' special. Since the first day you came through that door. You lit this place up. Like some kinda angel. It just ain't gonna be the same without you."

Awww. That's sweet.

"I'm gonna miss you too, Houston. You really are a sweet man." I kiss him on the cheek.

He quickly says, "But don't let it get around."

I smile at that.

Charles, on the porch of Nellie's restaurant, is waiting for Adam and me to arrive. The whole Ingalls clan comes out to greet us as the stagecoach pulls up.

Across the road, Mrs. Oleson has gone into business with a land speculator by the name of Edgar Mills, who has set up a small company selling shares in a big stretch of land he bought up north.

Adam says, "I've never seen this town so fired up."

And Charles replies, "Somethin' about the smell of easy money. It does get folks excited."

Even Reverend Alden thinks "it's a good investment for the church."

Dr. Baker wants to think it over. Smart man.

We have dinner with the family at the Little House, and we talk excitedly about our new office, which is conveniently located just above the post office in town. We'll be living there, as well, at least for the time being.

Our new office/home is ready. Adam hangs up his shingle, and we are officially open for business. As if on cue, there is a knock on the door. It is Nels Oleson, and it's not just a social call. He is our first client! Nels is concerned about the fact that the whole town seems to be withdrawing their savings from the bank and buying on credit at the Mercantile, just so they can invest in this land development scheme.

He tells Adam and me, "I don't want to find that I've got a lot of unpaid bills."

"Do you think it's a fraud?" I ask.

To which Nels responds, "Probably not."

"Well, exactly what is it that bothers you?" Adam inquires.

"Well, if that property is so valuable and he owns all of it, seems to me he oughta keep the profits—instead of selling shares."

No wonder Nels is such a good businessman.

Adam asks him, "Do you know if the land has been surveyed?"

Nels shakes his head. "No. Harriet told me to mind my own business when I asked about that."

"Well, it shouldn't be too hard to check. I'll just make a phone call."

That Adam's a smart guy, too.

Nels seems relieved and says, "Good. I feel better already."

In the meantime Edgar Mills has stopped selling shares. "I can't sell what I don't have," he says. But Mrs. O. has offered to sell some of her shares to Doc Baker—at ten percent over cost.

Naturally.

The next morning, Dr. Baker rides in like a man possessed. Nels asks him what's wrong? Doc jumps out of the buggy and growls, "We've been swindled, that's what's the trouble!" He goes into the restaurant and announces that he has just come back from up north and has seen their land: "We don't own land. We *own* a lake."

He and these townspeople climb the stairs of the hotel to see Mills and get their money back. Mills tells them, "I had no idea it would flood."

Uh. Huh.

They make a citizen's arrest and lock him in the ice house. What are they planning to do—freeze him to death? Mills asks to see Adam. He would like Adam to represent him.

Adam protests, "A lot of my friends got hurt from this little scheme of yours. I'm a member of *their* community."

Mills goes on: "The idea was that a man is innocent until proven guilty, but apparently that doesn't work here."

"Of course it does."

"Then for God's sake, help me, man. Are you a *lawyer* or not? Mr. Kendall, I need you."

That night Adam is awake—thinking. He wakes me, tells me that he's "gonna take the case."

"Mary, I'm a lawyer. And it's my job to defend him—no matter what my personal feelings are."

The next day, Adam talks with Charles at the Mill. Charles tells him that news travels fast and that "folks aren't too happy about it."

Adam says, "I've already given my word."

" 'Suppose a man has to do what he has to do," Charles responds.

Adam is about to receive his first verbal threat. A man named Jed says, "Well, you might reconsider, boy. You're makin' a big mistake."

Adam replies, "You know, I'm a little too old for you to be calling me boy. And if it's a mistake, I guess it's mine to make."

Yay! Good for you, Adam!

But it seems that Jed will no longer do business with Charles or our family. That night, there's another first: Rocks are thrown through our window! We are scared, but this does not deter Adam. The trial takes place at the Courthouse in Sleepy Eye. Edgar Mills is on the stand. The prosecutor asks if he is familiar with a Thomas W. Harcourt—a surveyor by profession?

Mills nods. "I know him."

The prosecutor continues, "This is a copy of the confidential report to Mr. Edgar Mills that the land that he had already purchased was worthless."

Adam wants the earth to open up and swallow him, hearing all this, and he says, "If it please the court, I'd like a little time to re-assess my position—if indeed, I have one."

Adam visits his client in jail: "Why didn't you tell me? We could've put in a guilty plea and asked for mercy."

Mills is looking at eighteen years in prison, and all he can say is, "I'm sorry."

Adam tells him that maybe, "if you return what's left of the money, that could save you maybe ten."

Mills replies, "It's gone. Spent. I owed some money, Mr. Kendall. I appreciate your concern, but it's over. I'm ready for any punishment that the court deems necessary."

That night we are discussing the issue.

"Oh, Mary. My first case. My client *lies* to me. Then he won't even give me a chance to help him out."

"Adam, you can't blame yourself for what happened."

"Dear God, Mary, he's gonna spend the rest of his life in prison, and he doesn't even seem to care."

There is a knock at the door. Adam opens it to find a man who claims to be Edgar Mills's physician, along with Mills's wife and young son. Mrs. Edna Mills was played by Barbara Collentine (Richard Bull's wife).

Adam ushers them inside and tells them that when he asked about relatives to contact, Mills said he was a widower without any family.

The doctor goes on to explain that he saw an article on land fraud and learned about the trial. After reading this article, Dr. Ruddy then went to Mrs. Mills with information that Edgar had sworn him not to disclose. However, in this case, the doctor felt it was his duty to divulge the truth.

The next day, court is in session.

Adam says, "Your honor, we would like to call Mrs. Edgar Mills to the stand."

Edgar objects to this and says, "I'm guilty!"

He does *not* want his wife to testify, but Edna ignores his outburst.

"Dr. Ruddy told me that my husband had only a few more months to live," Edna says. She goes on to say that they have three children. They have lived frugally, week to week, until recently.

"My husband sent me bank drafts every day. I deposited them in the bank. He told me that his ship had finally come in."

Adam addresses the jury: "Gentlemen of the jury. We are not in any way trying to evade my client's guilt. What we are saying is that you consider the circumstances behind his actions."

After he learned about his physical condition, he panicked. He needed to make money—and quick.

Later that day, the jury is in, and people are filing back into the court-room. The same Judge Adams from previous episodes is presiding over the courtroom. This role was played by the late character actor, John Zaremba, whose bio goes on forever. Mike knew him from *Bonanza*, but the rest of us knew him as the "Hills Bros. Coffee Man" from the famous commercials of the 70s and 80s. Mike talked with him about that, asking how the company got away with calling him a coffee expert, when he was just playing one on TV. Mike was a stickler for truth in advertising. He used to complain that there were green popsicles shown on the box, but not a single one in sight once you opened it. Speaking of commercials, we once filmed at a turkey ranch with tons of live turkeys running around and gobbling. When we needed quiet, the turkeys weren't listening. They continued gobbling. Mike suddenly let out an unbelievably shrill whistle, and you better believe those turkeys stood at attention. Silence. Mike filmed this and sent it to E.F. Hutton, whose slogan at that time was, "When E.F. Hutton talks, everybody listens." Unfortunately, they didn't see the humor in it. Too bad.

Anyway, back to the jury's verdict: Guilty of fraud. But the judge says that Mrs. Mills has pledged to return all of the money that's left.

He continues, saying, "Mr. Mills, I have here a list of the names of people whom you defrauded." He explains that the individuals on the list have each made pledges to the court. For example, Mrs. Oleson plans to employ Mills's wife in exchange for room and board. "And Dr. Baker has pledged medical attention to your family for as long as they live in Walnut Grove, and the list goes on."

"Mr. Mills—you see, these people who became involved in your scheme out of greed now wish to become involved with your family out of compassion. It appears that many have learned a great deal about themselves from this case."

Lastly, Judge Adams says, "You are to live out the remainder of your days in the comfort and love of your family."

I give Adam a congratulatory hug, and I'm wearing those gloves!

Mr. Davis, the blowhard, walks up and barks, "Kendall! That was a heck of a job," to which Adam replies, "Thank you."

Mr. Davis wants to have a meeting because, "I think there's a very good chance I can find a spot for you in my law firm."

"I'm very sorry, but I think my partner and I would rather go it alone," Adam proudly says.

"Look, son. I can make you a much better offer than anything your partner can afford."

"No, I don't think you can." Adam looks at me and says, "Let's go to lunch, partner."

SEASON EIGHT
May 1981–January 1982

CHAPTER NINETEEN

"A Christmas They Never Forgot" and Where *Pigeons Go to Die*

"The Reincarnation of Nellie," Parts 1 and 2 were written and directed by Mike. Definitely not his best work, as you can probably tell from the title.

When popular television series begin to run out of steam and are past their prime, especially after many years, they often resort to some common, albeit cheap, tricks to try and squeeze out another couple of years. Mike was not above this kind of thing. He brought in two new young kids to live with the Ingalls: Jason Bateman (*Arrested Development*) as James and Missy Francis as Cassandra, a pseudo-Laura character—braids and all. The writers would thread many old storylines into new episodes in the hope of keeping *Little House* the big hit it had previously been.

As I witnessed some of this desperation, I was even more sure of my decision to leave. I would be going out on a high note rather than letting the ratings dwindle and have the show cancelled by the network—which was ultimately what happened during the following year.

In this episode, Nellie and her husband, Percival, have traveled back East to visit his ailing father. Unfortunately, his father dies and Percival feels that, as the only son, it is his responsibility to take over the business for the sake of the rest of the family. Harriet is beside herself. She misses Nellie and her grandchildren so.

Nels tells Caroline, "You can't keep your children with you forever. It's just that New York—it's so far."

Adam and I have our own bad news to break to Ma and Pa. Adam can't make a living in Walnut Grove and is going to work at his father's old firm in . . . New York. A popular place—even back then!

Adam tells them, "I wouldn't go unless I had to."

And Pa replies, "I know. I'm happy for you. You've studied hard. It's not right that you're not able to use your abilities to their fullest."

Ma chimes in, "Course not. From what I hear, folks in the city sue each other every day."

She abruptly gets up to make more coffee. I try to comfort her as Adam goes outside with Charles.

Caroline is overwhelmed at her job at Nellie's restaurant. She can't handle everything on her own without Harriet's help. Nels decides to close it down until Harriet is in a better place emotionally and can come back to work. The phone rings. Hester-Sue is calling to tell us that she no longer works at the School for the Blind. The State has taken it over and insists that she get her teaching credential if she wants to stay on. Hester-Sue can't imagine going back to school at her age, so she leaves. Caroline immediately jumps in, offering her the restaurant job. Hester-Sue accepts and will come to Walnut Grove tomorrow.

Problem solved.

Dr. Baker has been to see Mrs. Oleson, who is in a deep depression. She says she has "nothing to live for."

As he talks with Nels, Baker has an idea and queries, "Have you ever given any thought to adopting a child?"

Nels shakes his head, says, "No."

Dr. Baker continues, saying that the Olesons are both healthy and in good shape financially. "At your age, I wouldn't recommend an infant, but orphanages are filled with girls nine, ten years old. Only a thought . . ."

The wheels are turning in Nels's head. "Yeah, yeah. Thanks, Doc."

He has hope.

We hear sad music (from "I'll be Waving As You Drive Away," to be exact) over a wide shot of the Post Office with the rooms above it in which Adam and I lived and worked. Uh, oh. It must be time. Yep. We are about to leave Walnut Grove for good and are saying our goodbyes.

Hester-Sue says goodbye to me with a big hug.

Laura hugs me and says, "I'll use my Braille Writer so Adam can't read my letters."

Pa's turn: "Don't you go lettin' those city folks change you too much, alright?"

"I won't. I'll eat with my shoes off at least once a week."

We hug and he says, "I love ya."

And I reply, "I love you, too."

Mike and I weren't acting in this scene—we *did* love each other and knew we were going to miss working together after seven-plus years. My face was wet from all those tears; my nose was running. It was hard to say goodbye.

I move to Ma as she says, "I won't cry, and I won't say goodbye."

We embrace, and I sob, "I love you, Ma."

"Well, at least I won't say goodbye." She kisses me on both cheeks—the way I kiss *my* daughter—and says, "Get along now, you've got two thousand and one miles to go."

We climb aboard the stagecoach and set off.

Dr. Baker tells Charles that Harriet didn't much like his adoption idea. Charles wonders if bringing Cassandra (who was herself adopted) might help cheer Harriet up and open her mind a bit, as well? Dr. Baker thinks that might just work.

Soon after, Charles brings Cassandra to spend some time with Mrs. O., and before long, the little girl is reading her a story and we see her spirits lifted. It has worked. Mrs. Oleson is back to her old, cranky self and even asks Nels to take her to Sleepy Eye to look around one of the orphanages there.

At an orphanage, Mrs. O. hasn't seen any girls who live up to her memory of young Nellie. Nels says, "Harriet, you can't expect to find someone exactly like Nellie," and they start down the hallway to leave.

Suddenly, we hear CRASH! BANG! And a high-pitched voice shrieking, "I hate you! I hate all of you!"

The head of the orphanage, Mr. Case, says, "*That* is Nancy. She is an incorrigible child, and we just can't handle her."

He goes to the door from which all of the commotion has come, opens it, and is head-butted straight back against the wall. The little girl turns and runs.

Harriet says, "That's her!"

Mr. Case says weakly, "That's who?"

"That's my Nellie! Stop her, Nels!"

And a chase ensues. Nancy followed by Nels and Nels by Harriet. Nancy runs into a shop, tells the men in there that a man is *chasing* her. Nels runs in, saying he's "trying to catch a little girl!"

POW!! A quick jab lands right on the old kisser, and poor Nels is down. Harriet catches Nancy as she comes out of the shop, but the girl bites her hard and is off.

Harriet says, "Get her, Nels!"

"Yes, my love."

Richard Bull was so good as Mr. Oleson. He always made it look so easy. Believe me, it wasn't.

Nels finds the girl hiding among many wooden crates. He turns quickly and captures her inside one of them. Harriet is overjoyed and starts cooing and baby-talking to this terror of a child. Nancy sticks out an arm and punches Harriet in the nose.

Nels can only shake his head in disbelief.

"I was wrong, Harriet. There *is* another child exactly like Nellie."

Back inside the orphanage, Mr. Case says, "Mrs. Oleson, you have to face the fact that the child does not want to be adopted. Now,

I don't know her reasons, but she doesn't, and we can't force her to go with you."

Harriet is indignant. "But I want her."

The matron attempts to explain just what a terror this child has been, but Harriet merely shrugs and says, "Girls will be girls."

Nels thinks this little girl is a monster and says, "With all of these children in the orphanage, why her?"

To which Harriet replies, "I don't know, but I want her."

Nels sighs deeply. "I give up."

Harriet has made it her mission in life to change this girl's mind.

Mr. Case says, "She's wasting her time. That child will not go with her."

"I only hope you're right," Nels says.

Harriet tries to talk to Nancy through a locked door. She cajoles, pleads, but to no avail.

Trying a new tack, Harriet tells the child about Nellie. She decides to tell Nancy the truth.

"Children hated my Nellie because she was mean and spoiled— conniving. I understood that because I was exactly the same way when I was a child. So you see, I *do* understand *you*, Nancy. And you don't have to change. I'll love you just the way you are. And I'll spoil you with beautiful dresses and lovely big dolls and all the candy you can eat. And maybe, maybe, someday, maybe, you'll love me, too? Please, Nancy, please give me a chance. Give me a chance to be your mother." She sniffles. "Nancy, honey? Nancy?"

The door slowly opens. The girl comes out.

"Mother?"

The word Harriet has longed to hear.

"My Nancy."

The happy threesome arrives back in Walnut Grove.

Harriet goes to Willie and says, "Mother has a surprise for you."

She introduces the two kids, and Willie says, "This is my surprise?

We finally get Nellie married and out of the house, and you bring home another one!"

So now our writers can re-hash old Nellie plotlines for Nancy, and Walnut Grove will have a spoiled little rich girl once again.

Part 2 of the episode is predictable, with Nancy lying all the time and being as mean as possible. In the end, she gets hers—quite literally, in the Mermaid Dunking Booth at the school bazaar. The "Dunkee" was, of course, mean old Nancy.

Laura's narration ends with "We knew she'd still be nasty. But she'd be better. 'Cause she knew folks cared enough about her not to let her get away with things she shouldn't.'"

And then came the line that made my jaw drop:

"So just remember that the next time your folks punish you."

Say what?!

There is an unwritten rule in dramatic filmmaking that says, "Never break the Fourth Wall." This means, never look directly at the camera (because it will appear that you are looking at the audience) and never *talk* directly to the camera, for the same reason. This narration is breaking that rule because it is no longer storytelling and is really stupid, as well. I wonder if Melissa Gilbert questioned it during her looping session. Mike shouldn't have gotten away with that. And I can't believe it stayed in the final cut of the episode.

Amazing.

I shot *Advice to the Lovelorn*, an NBC Movie of the Week starring Cloris Leachman and got to team up with my old pal Lance Kerwin again. We had a good time as usual, and when it was finished, I went back to the Little House for my final episode.

"A Christmas They Never Forgot," I forgot—literally. And it's no wonder because I had exactly six lines, which were:

"Merry Christmas!"

"Then it wouldn't have been a surprise."

"Listen. Outside."

"We might not make it if we wait too long."

"Oh, Adam."

"Tell her the story, Ma. Adam hasn't heard it, either."

And then Mary goes to sleep and stays asleep for the rest of this episode.

Not great use of me or of Linwood Boomer in what was our last hurrah, so to speak. After all the fuss made about visiting being so difficult and New York being so far, I would have hoped for a much better send-off than this.

Oh, well.

That spring I flew to Jupiter, Florida, to perform in Neil Simon's *The Gingerbread Lady* at the Burt Reynolds Dinner Theater. I was taking Kirk Douglas's advice and getting my "theater chops." Boy, did I ever. After a few weeks of rehearsal with our director, Charles Nelson Reilly, we got to opening night and had no star. Hope Lange—remember her from *The Ghost and Mrs. Muir*?—was in the hospital in traction for a bad back or neck or both.

Mr. Burt Reynolds himself telephoned me in my dressing room to thank me for hanging in there to carry the show while Ms. Lange was out. What else *could* I do?

So I said, "You're welcome, Mr. Reynolds," and continued getting ready to open that night.

Everyone at the theater had been very supportive, including Dick Cavett, the comedian and talk show host, who was starring in the play after ours, *Charley's Aunt.* He was one of the smartest and funniest people I've ever met, and I enjoyed hanging out with him with the limited time we both had outside of my performances and his rehearsals.

The understudy went on holding the book (the play) in her hands but did a good job, and we got rave reviews. Eventually, Hope Lange came back, and we got into a groove and really had some fun.

The audiences seemed to like our show a lot, and I had my "baptism by fire" into theater.

For inspiration, and because I was scared out of my wits initially, I had this taped to the mirror in my dressing room at the theatre:

> I wanted to be an actress in 1912; I want to be
> an actress today. That walk from the darkness
> backstage through the door or opening in the
> scenery where I make an entrance into the bright
> lights with that big dim mass out beyond, which
> bursts into applause, then the first terrifying
> sound that comes out of my throat, which they
> describe as a voice, but that first instant it is the
> siren of terror and intention and faith and hope and
> trust and vanity and security and insecurity and
> bloodcurdling courage which is acting.
>
> —*Ruth Gordon (1896–1985)*

In May of 1982, I flew to Seattle to shoot a CBS Movie of the Week entitled, *A Innocent Love.* I was cast as Molly Rush, a college volleyball player, which was an interesting change of pace for me. I actually worked out with a college team and got a bit of the hang of being a setter in the game. The setter doesn't have to be tall necessarily, so at five-foot-four, that was a believable position for me to play.

Molly needed some help academically, so she enlisted a tutor in the form of a young genius kid played by Doug McKeon. I was excited when I found out that Doug would be co-starring in this movie. He was a great, young actor who had many years of experience. I had recently seen him in a TV movie *Daddy, I Don't Like It Like This* with Burt Young and thought he was amazing.

Doug and I hit it off and had a great time filming in rainy, but sooo green Seattle. We shot at the University of Washington, where Doug filmed his rowing scenes as part of the "crew," and I played volleyball with the girls there. That was fun—they said I wasn't *that* bad!

We worked hard and did good work. The movie turned out well and was a hit ratings-wise. Doug and I remain friends to this day.

I filmed yet another TV Movie of the Week, *First Affair*, in Boston, Massachusetts. I played a young co-ed babysitter who falls hard for her married employer. In the film, my character Toby (a better name for a cat than a girl!) is enrolled at Harvard, and we actually shot the movie on campus. Fun! Even better was the fact that my two best friends, Pam and Tam, were able to work as extras in the movie, so we got to spend a lot of time together that summer.

I made my second feature film, *Chattanooga Choo Choo*, co-starring Barbara Eden (*I Dream of Jeannie*), George Kennedy, and Joe Namath. Sometimes one makes the decision to take a part based more on the part than the entire project. I liked this role and the movie was . . . cute. The best thing about this film was meeting one of my closest friends, Ellen, who played one of the cheerleaders in the movie.

During the next couple of years, I worked a lot for my friend Aaron Spelling. We were not close personal friends, but we did so much work together, I considered him my friend.

He hired me to guest-star in two-part episodes of his many TV series, a couple of pilots, and finally a two-hour *Love Boat* cruise. This was what I had been afraid of. I liked shooting my *Love Boat*s on the lot at Fox. Close to home, convenient. I didn't like the idea of being stuck out in the middle of the ocean with nowhere to go, no escape. But as I had already done three episodes all shot on land, I really had to say yes and venture out onto the high seas for this one.

It wasn't so bad to spend three weeks aboard a beautiful luxury liner cruising around the Mediterranean. Mine was the Italy, Spain, Portugal leg, and it *was* lovely, especially when we docked and I could get off and tour the cities a bit. Italy and Spain were my favorites. I had visited Madrid while doing publicity for *Little House*, but this time, I saw Barcelona—beautiful. I even saw real bullfighting, which was exciting and horrifying at the same time. I traveled to Milan, but not being a "fashion connoiseur," I didn't appreciate it quite as much as the other Italian cities I have visited. Writing this is making me look even more forward to an upcoming European vacation I have planned with my son. Working in exotic locales is interesting; moreover, it's a great way to scout out the places you love the most and want to go back to one day on a real vacation.

In the '80s, I got my name back! When I first started acting, I was billed as "Melissa Anderson" until I found out that there was *another* Melissa Anderson in Screen Actors Guild. She did not seem to work, but she paid her dues and therefore, had first rights to that name. I added my middle name at that time, but I never liked it. I thought it sounded very young, and people were always calling me Melissa Sue instead of just Melissa. I don't know what happened to the other Melissa Anderson, but I was very happy to be notified that I could finally have the name I wanted.

One day in 1986, I received a call from my agent asking if I might be interested in portraying Edward Woodward's daughter in the CBS hit drama, *The Equalizer*. That was one of those moments that are so few and far between in this business. I was over the moon! I absolutely *loved* that show, and to think I was being asked to be a part of it, just thrilled me. And with such respect, as well: They simply called, asked about my availability, and offered me the role. I immediately said yes, of course I'd be interested, and waited with great anticipation for my first two-part scripts to be delivered for my final "okay."

These episodes entitled "Memories of Manon" were well-crafted by Coleman Luck and director Tony Wharmby. I have recently gotten back in touch with *novelist* Coleman Luck, and we both look back fondly at that *Equalizer* time and with great pride.

For me, working in New York on that show was perfection. This was my dream job. The hours were long, the weather could be cruel, but I didn't care. I had never had so much fun in my whole life. I loved this city; my best friend, Pam, was there. I would meet her after work, or she'd visit me on the set. I couldn't have been happier. And the work I was doing was (hopefully) as good as the material I had to work with. That was the best part: these episodes were so smart, so interesting and dramatic. Any actor's dream.

After having the time of my life shooting those first two episodes, I got to look forward to the next season and my next two-parter, "The Mystery of Manon." It was at this time that I received an offer to fly to Toronto to shoot the first episode of the new *Alfred Hitchcock Presents* series that was shooting up there. It seemed that there was some problem getting me an entire script to read in order to make a decision, yes or no. My agent had seen some pages, which she read to me over the phone. Who would have thought, back in the late eighties, that all of these logistical difficulties could be so simply cured with the broader use of the computer? I tell my kids how lucky they are—all of that research right at their fingertips. Okay, I give up. I *am* old. Anyway, my agent happened to mention that this "Very Careful Rape" episode was written and executive-produced by Michael Sloan who, by the way, created *The Equalizer*. Well, *that* changed things. Okay, I thought. I can risk this. This guy's track record is great. He's a really good writer, and we know how I felt about *The Equalizer*, so I jumped on board.

I left for Toronto the following morning and was handed my script as I climbed into the Town Car that would take me to the airport. I read the script, loved it, and started learning my dialogue on the flight. I should tell you, Michael Sloan is not known for writing communicative looks, glances. He writes dialogue. Lots and *lots* of dialogue. It's always good and there's always tons of it to learn. I remember commiserating with Edward Woodward about that. He knew Michael from way back and had worked with him even before *The Equalizer. He* knew what I was talking about.

On the flight to Toronto, I met the Canadian executive producer, Jon Slan. He was super-nice and even quizzed me on some of my dialogue. This was a good omen, I thought. So far, so good.

It was a good thing I had been going to my exercise classes at Nautilus Plus regularly because this Universal production team really liked to eat, and, will wonders never cease, they included *me* in these gastronomic adventures. The only other time I had ever dined with my producers while shooting was on that *Love Boat* cruise. We actors ate with Doug Kramer (the other executive producer with Aaron) on a couple of occasions. So this was pretty new for me and pretty fun, too.

I worked really hard every day on this episode but was rewarded by being invited out each evening. I got to know Michael Sloan during these dinners, and we definitely hit it off. One of the other producers, Nigel Watts, an Englishman and dapper dresser, liked the idea of the two of us together. He said, "You each have two dogs, you're both Libras, and Missy has the same birthday as your late father, Michael."

The Elegant Matchmaker, I called him.

Michael and I had a lot in common except for the fact that he was from a show business family and I was not. Michael's maternal grandfather, Fred Stone, had starred on Broadway in the premiere production of *The Wizard of Oz.* And Michael himself started out as an actor and had, in his words, "such an illustrious career that I became a writer." So, we were a good team. He (almost) fit my criteria for the perfect mate:

1. A good sense of humor. Check.
2. A good measure of success. Check.

3. A "suit." I always thought I should be with a guy who wore a suit. Michael wore a jacket. Half a check. Nobody's perfect. Oh, and he is tall, too. There's the other half. Done.

I flew back to New York for my second two-part "Equalizer: The Mystery of Manon." This story was even better than the first two hours, I thought. We hit a rough patch, though, shooting at night in the freezing, and I mean *freezing,* cold. I believe the weatherman said 7 degrees Fahrenheit—yep, that was about what it felt like.

Edward nicely invited me into his motor home to get out of the cold. I had one, as well, but his was closest, and I could tell that he wanted to talk. We ran our lines, and we talked and talked. We discovered we had a mutual friend in Michael Sloan. Although he had created *The Equalizer,* Michael was no longer actively participating in the day-to-day workings of the show. I didn't realize how far back Edward's and Michael's friendship went; Edward didn't know Michael and I had been dating. Edward decided to give Michael Sloan a call.

```
EXT. UNIVERSAL STUDIOS - LATE AFTERNOON
- ESTABLISHING

CAMERA TIGHTENS ONTO a white pyramid building
across from the Black Tower, 3rd floor.


INT. MICHAEL SLOAN'S OFFICE - LATE AFTERNOON

MICHAEL is working on a script. His door opens and
his Secretary, SUSAN BRANDES, pokes her head in.

                  SUSAN BRANDES
        Edward Woodward, on line two, calling
        from New York.

Susan has never spoken to Edward Woodward before.
Michael is also surprised.
```

CONTINUED:

                    MICHAEL SLOAN
    Really!

Michael has not spoken to Edward in some time. He
picks up the phone receiver, punches line two.

                    MICHAEL SLOAN
         (into phone)
    Hi, Edward!

INTERCUT WITH EDWARD WOODWARD IN A NEW YORK CITY
BACK ALLEY AT NIGHT

Edward is sitting in his chair with the name
"EDWARD WOODWARD" stenciled on the back. Sitting beside him is Melissa, in her own chair, both
of them bundled up against the cold. The EQUAL-
IZER CREW is setting up the next shot around them.
Breath plumes from Edward's mouth as he clutches
the heavy cell-phone in a gloved hand. He speaks
in a clipped, London accent.

                  EDWARD WOODWARD
        (into cell phone)
    Michael! This is Edward. Woodward, you
    remember? "The Equalizer?" You cast me
    in this role?

                    MICHAEL SLOAN
        (a little unnerved)
    Of course, Edward. How are you?

                  EDWARD WOODWARD
    How am I? Well, before I answer that
    question, what's the temperature in
    Los Angeles right now?

                    MICHAEL SLOAN
    It's around eighty degrees, I guess.
    You know, the usual for L.A.

CONTINUED:

Edward glances significantly at Melissa.

> EDWARD WOODWARD
> Eighty degrees? Oh, that's nice.
> That's very nice. I'm sitting here in
> a dark alley in New York - Melissa
> Anderson is also here, by the way,
> says hi - well, she would, if she
> could speak, but her lips are blue
> — and it's 7 degrees here, Michael.
> *Seven*. And need I remind you, I have a
> *heart* condition.

> MICHAEL SLOAN
> Of course, Edward, I know that and I'm
> sorry to hear about the weather, but
> . . .

> EDWARD WOODWARD
> (right over him)
> And I am not about to shoot this next
> scene with Melissa. No, she's here
> to keep me company. She's in a later
> scene, poor girl. No, my co-actor in
> the next scene . . . is a wolf.
> Now, the wolf, Michael... the wolf
> is wearing a fur coat. So the wolf
> doesn't mind the bitter cold. But The
> Equalizer, you see, Michael, Robert
> McCall does not have a fur coat. Do
> you know why not?

Michael is smiling now; he loves Edward.

> MICHAEL SLOAN
> No, why is that, Edward?

> EDWARD WOODWARD
> Because you did not create a fur coat
> for him. I am wearing an overcoat. And

```
CONTINUED:

                    EDWARD WOODWARD (CON'T)
          gloves. You did do that for me. The
          Equalizer at least wears gloves. But
          when we get to this scene, Michael, I
          don't think an overcoat or gloves are
          going to save me from frostbite.

     Melissa is smiling now and there's a twinkle in
     Edward's eyes.

                    MICHAEL SLOAN
          Probably not.

                    EDWARD WOODWARD
          Just thought I'd let you know how your
          creation was faring here on the East
          Coast as you bask in the Los Angeles
          sunshine.

     And so it goes. But Michael and Edward are
     very happy to be talking to one another again
     and Melissa has enjoyed every moment of their
     conversation.
```

Michael and Edward hatched a plan wherein Michael would fly down to New York from Toronto and we could all have dinner— what else? We went to the Four Seasons and had a terrific time listening to Edward recount many, many hilarious stories of his days in the British theater. He had a gift as a raconteur. Unbeatable. He and his lovely wife, actress Michele Dotrice, made an adorable, not to mention, fun couple.

These *Equalizers* were little gems — top-notch television, really.

I was the only actress to star in two *Alfred Hitchcock Presents* episodes—but I had connections. Honestly, though, my first episode was very dark and dramatic and the very first of the season. By the time I was asked to do the second one, many months had passed, and I would be playing a funny, loquacious character completely different from the first.

I liked the character Julie Fenton so much that I wished I could have played her in a series. She reminded me of Marlo Thomas in *That Girl* and Elizabeth Montgomery in *Bewitched* all wrapped up into one funny girl. I talked incessantly in this episode. I (purposely) talked to the camera—right into everyone's living rooms! I sat and talked. I talked in bed. I walked and ran and talked all the while. Interestingly, the operator of the steadicam (hand-held and absolutely smooth camera) was this talented guy, Jon Cassar, who went on to great success as director and executive producer of *24*. I don't know how he did it, he had to walk backwards fast up and down stairs and all over this split-level home while I drove everyone nuts walking and talking a mile a minute. This episode turned out well. And funny. Even my son Griffin gets a kick out of it.

Michael and I occasionally socialized with Mike and Cindy Landon. We all lived in Malibu at that time and would get together for dinner in the neighborhood from time to time. I apologized to Cindy for giving her the cold shoulder all those years ago. She accepted and said that I wasn't the only one.

One night at BeauRivage, one of our local haunts, Michael and I pitched Mike Landon *Where Pigeons Go to Die*, a book written by our friend, Robert Campbell. We thought this material would be right up his alley.

Mike was very interested and wanted to read it right away. He called us as soon as he had, to let us know he wanted to produce it as a TV movie for NBC. We were happy to have our good friend, the late Bob Campbell, get some well-deserved worldwide attention paid to his heartwarming story. And Mike made me associate producer, which was a nice thing for me, as well.

Where Pigeons Go to Die aired on January 29, 1990, and Michael and I were married in a beautiful rooftop ceremony in Los Angeles on March 17. It was St. Patrick's Day, so I wore my emeralds, and my dad, very handsome in his tux, walked me down the aisle. Mike and Cindy were there, as well as Kent and Susan McCray and several others from my *Little House* family. Having those people there who had always meant so much to me helped to make my special day even more so.

Michele and Edward Woodward hosted our "Blessing" exactly one week later at Charingworth Manor in Gloucestershire, England. This was lovely, especially because Michael had many friends in the U.K. from his sixteen years spent living there. It was a breathtaking spot with no rain that day, just white billowy clouds. Another good omen.

Still superstitious after all those years.

Edward passed away on November 16th, 2009. We hadn't spoken to him or Michele recently, so it came as quite a shock. An unfortunate reminder of the frailty of life. Don't lose touch. Tell your friends how much they mean to you while you can.

CHAPTER TWENTY

Reflections

I am often asked what it was like to be a "child star?" What it was like to grow up on television? I hope that I've been able to answer those questions in this book.

When I look back at my life growing up, I can see plainly the many valuable experiences I had, the many things I learned—life lessons.

I was smart enough to realize how lucky I was and not to take it for granted. Success came early for me, but it was no less *earned* with many hours of hard work and perseverance.

I was an only child thrust into a family of one hundred cast and crew. I learned to be a team player. I understood that all of those people "had my back," and I appreciated each and every one of them. I learned that I was no better (and no worse) than anyone else.

My biggest regret would be that I didn't trust myself enough sooner. I wish I had believed in myself more. I wish I could have been a bit easier on myself—let myself off the hook occasionally. I had to act like an adult before my time, so I guess it stands to reason that I'd have to go back and catch myself up in certain areas.

I am not complaining. I am proud of what I accomplished and of the person that my *Little House* family was instrumental in helping me to become.

When Mike died on July 1st, 1991, *USA Today* called to ask me for a quote. I told them that he was "America's Family Man."

It was the truth.

TAG

After my stint as the Equalizer's daughter, I worked a bit more in TV Movies of the Week such as *The Return of Sam McCloud* and in another feature film, *Dead Men Don't Die,* co-starring Elliott Gould. I loved my character, Dulcie. The film itself? Pretty silly.

On February 15, 1991, Piper Kathleen Sloan was born, and my life was completely changed. Everyone says how great it is to have kids, but of course you never *really* know until it happens.

While I was pregnant, I decided that I would retire, at least for a while, working only occasionally for friends. I had worked hard for twenty years and thought I should take a break to concentrate on my child. I had never forgotten that "Magic Mountain moment" with the Landon kids. I wanted my child to be the one drawing the attention, not me.

I've been hearing interesting comments of late from some actors, talking about fatherhood. They mention how they were afraid they might have been too narcissistic to be good parents. I had those same reservations before Piper was born. Fortunately, as with these actors, once that tiny baby was actually in my arms, all of my protective, parenting instincts kicked in, and I need not have worried.

It's just possible that we actors make really *good* parents because we *are* so aware of our own shortcomings. We know what we *don't* want our children to be like.

The day after my little girl's first birthday, we flew up to Toronto so I could appear in the St. Lawrence Center for the Arts Theatre production of *To Grandmother's House We Go* for a good friend of ours, director John Wood. No major catastrophes occurred during those six weeks, but "Pippy Doodle" pulled herself up to standing and, as I reached the end of the run, she took her very first steps. Wow.

In 1994, I worked for Aaron Spelling once again, this time in an episode of *Burke's Law.*

Griffin Henry Sloan was born on June 14th, 1996. He had a full head of hair the color of an old penny—and an old soul to match. I was having a great time with these kids. I found it so interesting seeing the differences between my little girl and baby boy.

At six months, Griffy discovered "wheels." We could get him to do just about anything as long as he had a car or truck or train in his pudgy little hands.

And Piper loved nothing more than to give "parties" for all of her little Disney figures. She would line them all up, having long conversations with each one, and spend the rest of her day celebrating with them.

In 1998, I played a seismologist in *Earthquake in New York,* written and executive produced by Michael Sloan. I worked alongside Michael Moriarty, whose acting I had always admired, and Greg Evigan—who I knew personally but had never worked with.

I filmed *10.5 Apocalypse,* a four-hour mini-series for NBC in 2006, portraying the First Lady of the United States. Who would have thunk? It was a very good experience, and I started to toy with the idea of working more in the future. My kids were getting older; I'd be obsolete before I knew it.

I spent lots of time researching colleges, majors, etc., with my daughter in 2008, and I was so glad I had the time in which to do it. That has been such a luxury for me—the time to help with homework or bake cookies for the class at the very last minute. I was particularly happy to be of help to Piper because I knew that she'd get into some of these schools and be gone, living the college life—no Mom in sight. Well, it happened. She did get in and she *is* gone, but we talk every day, without exception. Of everything I've done in my life, I have loved my "Mom" gig the most. It is by far the best experience I've ever had—not to mention the hardest.

The timing of this book couldn't have been better for me. It has kept me busy (that's an understatement!) during this transitional year. It has also kept me from smothering my son, Griff, with too much attention—not exactly what a thirteen-year-old boy really wants. And after 70,000 words, I should definitely have an edge at the next Sloan family Scrabble game.

Filmography

The Handyman	Co-Star and Split Story Writing Credit, 2010
10.5 Apocalypse	NBC Mini-Series, 2006
Earthquake in New York	FOX FAMILY MOW, 1998
Burke's Law	ABC, 1994
Dead Men Don't Die	Feature Film, 1990
Where Pigeons Go To Die	NBC MOW as Associate Producer, 1990
Return of Sam McCloud	CBS MOW, 1989
The Equalizer	CBS, 1987–1988
Dark Mansions	ABC MOW/PILOT, 1986
The Love Boat	ABC (4 Episodes), 1978–1986
Chattanooga Choo Choo	Feature Film, 1984
First Affair	CBS MOW, 1983
An Innocent Love	CBS MOW, 1982
Little House on the Prairie	NBC, 1974–1981
Advice to the Lovelorn	NBC MOW, 1981
Happy Birthday to Me	Feature Film, 1981
Midnight Offerings	ABC MOW, 1981
Insight	1980
Fantasy Island	ABC, 1980
Which Mother is Mine?	ABC Afterschool Special, 1979
The Survival of Dana	CBS MOW, 1979

James at 15	NBC MOW, 1977
Very Good Friends	ABC Afterschool Special, 1977
The Loneliest Runner	NBC MOW, 1976
Little House on the Prairie	NBC MOW/PILOT, 1974
Shaft	NBC, 1973
Brady Bunch	ABC, 1973

Acknowledgments

This book would never have been written if not for Laura Dail's persistent belief that I *did* have a story to tell and that I *could* write this memoir. I truly appreciate her help all the way through this interesting, fun, and arduous experience.

I am grateful to Erin Turner at Globe Pequot. I learned so much from her insightful edits, and I valued her opinions. I thank her for trusting my vision along the way.

To my new friend, photographer Heidi Hollinger, for shooting the prettiest pictures of me.

To my husband, whose writing I've always admired, I thank him for playing the role of "typist" in my story. God only knows how long it would have taken me to hunt and peck my way through these twenty-plus chapters!

About the Author

Actress and first-time author Melissa Anderson lives in Montreal, Quebec, Canada, with her husband and two children.